Endorsements

"*From Survival to Success* is a must-read for every volunteer, bi-vocational, part-time or full-time worship leader, or minister of music. Daniel Morris combines stories from his own journey with common sense leadership principles to deliver a packed resource for any sized ministry organization."

—Cliff Duren
Worship Leader, Song Writer, Arranger, Orchestrator
Brentwood Baptist Church, Brentwood, Tennessee

"As a professor of church music and dean of a school of music and ministry studies, *From Survival to Success* will be on my required textbooks list. While there is a wealth of materials regarding worship in the twenty-first century, it is refreshing that this book is not that! I know students will find that this book is practical, thought-provoking, and full of ideas for a variety of music and worship ministries.

Daniel has done a masterful job of providing the kind of information that is often difficult to find today. The 'nuts and bolts' of church music administration is often a missing link in the training of church music professionals. As a church musician who has been doing this since 1974, I am pleased to recommend this book to the seasoned professional and my students will certainly be spending time with this text!"

—Dr. Don Odom
Dean, Winters School of Music and Ministry Studies
William Carey University, Hattiesburg, Mississippi

"In this book, Daniel Morris provides practical and strategic guidance for you as a worship leader. *From Survival to Success* will strengthen your personal life and enhance your ministry. Teach it and you will advance your effectiveness and multiply your leaders."

—Dr. Johnny Hunt
Senior Pastor
First Baptist Woodstock, Woodstock, Georgia

"The book you hold in your hand is a treasure for personal and professional growth. *From Survival to Success* is full of wisdom and practical insight forged in a unique environment of opportunity and from a commitment to learning, hard work, and passionate prayer. Read it, apply it, teach it, and share it. It will enrich your personal and family life, expand your ministry and broaden your influence. My joy and reward is Daniel Morris—who he has become and what he has accomplished—and what he yet will."

—Dr. Gary L. Crawford
Pastor, Author, Executive Coach
GaryCrawfordLeadership.com

"Wow! *From Survival to Success* is inspiring, encouraging, and instructional! As a business leader, I found the leadership principles in this book practical and impactful for my everyday life. This book is a must-read for anyone on a journey to success."

—Tony Bridwell
Partner, Partners In Leadership, Inc.

"Striking a balance between encouraging and admonishing, Daniel's heart and concern for his fellow worship pastor is evident in his writing. Through the vulnerability he shows in his writing, he pulls the curtain back on his own flaws and weaknesses in both his personal and ministerial life, to bring a fresh insight into topics that are ever pressing, yet rarely discussed publicly. 'Heart' chapters covering topics such as integrity, accountability, and spiritual development are paired flawlessly with 'Mind' chapters on communications, systems development, and volunteer deployment to create a manual for effective ministry. Whether you are starting out in ministry or just need a time of refreshment and refocusing of your ministry, *From Survival to Success* is a *must* for your library!"

—John W. Jennings
Vice President, Prism Music Inc., Franklin, Tennessee

From SURVIVAL
To SUCCESS

DANIEL MORRIS

From SURVIVAL To SUCCESS

PRACTICAL INSIGHTS
FOR WORSHIP MINISTRY
LEADERSHIP

TATE PUBLISHING
AND ENTERPRISES, LLC

Published by Tate Publishing & Enterprises, LLC
127 E. Trade Center Terrace | Mustang, Oklahoma 73064 USA
1.888.361.9473 | www.tatepublishing.com

Tate Publishing is committed to excellence in the publishing industry. The company reflects the philosophy established by the founders, based on Psalm 68:11,
"The Lord gave the word and great was the company of those who published it."

Book design copyright © 2016 by Tate Publishing, LLC. All rights reserved.
Cover design by Samson Lim
Interior design by Mary Jean Archival
Original manuscript edit by Fran Terhune

Published in the United States of America

ISBN: 978-1-68301-272-6
1. Religion / Christian Life / Professional Growth
2. Religion / Christian Ministry / Discipleship
16.02.16

Acknowledgments

To MY WIFE, Carolyn Morris, I have no words that could adequately describe the love I have for you, Carolyn. You have been my constant source of stability, honesty, and enablement. You always come alongside me and keep me out of trouble in all our crazy adventures. I would not be the man and minister I am today if not for your unselfish devotion to our shared ministry. You are my rare and precious jewel, and I am honored to lead and love with you.

To my children—Gray, Turner, and Jett—I want you to read this book one day and know that I have such a deep love and passion for the Lord and His church. But I also want you to know that you have always been and always will be my greatest ministry calling. I am so blessed to have you as my children.

To my mentor, Tony Bridwell, this is all your fault! If it were not for your encouragement, I would have never typed the first word of this book. I can't believe you took a chance on me. Your wonderful mentorship has turned into a deep friendship that I cherish. You have always believed in me and championed me for greater things. Now it is time for me to pay it forward. *Onward*!

To a great leader and friend, Dr. Gary Crawford, much of the inspiration for this book is birth out of the environment that you have given your ministry life to make possible. I have been challenged and enriched by our friendship and shared ministry.

I am a better leader because of your wonderful example for so many years.

To my parents, Harold and Barbara Morris, I just want to say thank-you for always believing in me and raising me to believe that I could do anything through Christ. I have never doubted your support and love for me. All I can say is, you did right by me, and I am grateful.

There is not a day that goes by that I am not influenced in some way by your enduring example of faithful dedication and service to the Lord.

Contents

Foreword

I RECEIVED A phone call one day in 2013 from the worship pastor at Westside Baptist Church in Gainesville, FL. It didn't take me long to realize that I was speaking with a man of God who was very intentional about his walk with the Lord and passionate about a calling that God had placed on his life. It was not until several months later that I realized how serious he also was about sock fashion. But more on that later...

By the end of that first conversation, he already had a flight booked for him and his staff to come visit in Nashville for a few days...mainly just so we could get to know one another and dream about some things that he wanted to see happen in the months ahead at his church. I was so impressed with his way of thinking and approach to music ministry...not afraid to be out of the box or strive for something beyond what had been done before in his ministry. I hung up the phone and thought, "Wow! How have I not known this guy before now?!" I knew then that I had just met someone who was going to teach me a lot. I also gained a great friend that day.

That was my first time ever speaking with Daniel Morris, but, thankfully, there have been many encouraging conversations since then.

I took a trip to Gainesville a few months later to do a weekend retreat with his choir. You can learn a lot about a worship pastor by hanging out with the folks under his leadership. I left that weekend with even more respect for Daniel and the incredible job he was doing. He had a strong ministry, but their strength was matched by their understanding of the importance of worship and their role as worship leaders.

Also, they straight-up LOVED their worship pastor.

Fast-forward a few more months, and I took another trip to Gainesville to experience a Sunday of worship services at Westside Baptist. In the Lord's perfect timing, Daniel's wife, Carolyn, gave birth to their third kiddo on Saturday evening. Needless to say, my plans changed that weekend and I filled in for Daniel by leading worship in his place.

This is when I learned even more about Daniel's leadership skills. Aside from familiarizing myself with the songs and arrangements for the worship services, my only role was to show up and focus on leading worship. Daniel had such effective systems in place that *everyone* involved knew their role and what was expected of them that morning. He had delegated so well to his trusted staff and lay-leaders that there was nothing for me to say and no instructions for me to give. I can honestly say that it was one of the easiest Sundays I have ever had as a worship leader…which is why I needed to read this book more than anyone!

I realize that, so far, this feels like a forward for Daniel's autobiography (Maybe I can write the forward for that one as well. I think the book should be called "Daniel Morris: The Man, the Calling, the Socks.") Every word written up until this point is to justify why Daniel needed to write this book. He knows what he is doing. He is not going to spend the pages of this book talking about things he is not already doing himself. These are not just great ideas. They are great practices.

Daniel has the humility to know why his music ministry functions at such a high level; he is counting on the Holy Spirit to do the work! Daniel is careful to begin this book by talking about the importance of the spiritual disciplines and their foundational role for any Christian leader. Then, as a husband and father, he is intentional to walk through some very practical ways to keep your family in their rightful place of priority. Finally, the remaining chapters are absolutely loaded with great insights for worship pastors at any stage of ministry. I was able to glean so much from this book as someone who has been in ministry for over 15 years. I cannot imagine the impact it will have on the worship pastor who is just getting started.

If you are an under-liner, you should probably grab a few extra pens. This booked is packed with solid content and numerous takeaways. I found myself challenged, convicted, and encouraged to sharpen and reexamine my own methods as a worship pastor. I have a feeling you will feel the same way.

Thank you, Daniel, for following the Holy Spirit's leading and writing this book. Also, thanks for being the only person who has ever sent me designer socks in the mail for no reason.

—Cliff Duren

Preface

I HAVE TAKEN a risk in using the word *success* in the title of this book. *Success* in our culture can be defined in ways that are unbecoming of a follower of Christ. *Success* has the potential to seem arrogant and therefore ungodly. But *success* is not an ungodly word. In fact, Christ died so that we can live life in abundance and success, as He defines these words in His teaching. So this raises the question, What do I mean by *success*? It is certainly not intended to mean that we have arrived or figured everything out. In fact, I am sure that shortly after this book is written, there will be some things that I will have changed my mind about slightly. Life experiences have a distinct way of shaping our ideas about ministry and what success looks like.

We do not have to apologize for wanting to live successful lives and have successful, life-changing ministries. But we must understand that there is no success in life or ministry outside of obedience and service to Jesus Christ. So my working definition of *success* from the perspective of this writing is to intentionally and effectively make a difference in people's lives on a regular basis with purpose, passion, thoughtfulness, organization, obedience, and wisdom.

The intention of this book is to give some practical leadership insights and principles that I am learning on my own journey that may help others live a life of influence and success in helping people worship and serve the Lord. We are not living in abundance and with a capacity to lead others well if we are just surviving and treading water in our lives and ministries. God has called us to something greater!

We all know what survival mode looks like. In survival mode, we only do what it takes to make it through another workday. Worship planning is minimum and quick, rehearsals are off-the-cuff, and family time is whatever is left over once our poorly planned day has come to an end. Survival mode means working hard all day with very little to show for it.

No one gains maximum benefit from the minister who is just surviving. There is more to ministry; there is a greater place of influence and significance. God wants us to live successfully, not just get by week after week. In this book, I offer practical steps that ministers of music, worship leaders, bandleaders, and other church staff members can take to move from a ministry of survival to a ministry of success.

The book is written for those who are serious about growing their ministry. The information will be most helpful to those who desire to build, serve, grow, change, and be challenged. All of us are looking for the definitive secret to ministry success. We try applying the latest gimmick or technique, hoping that it will be the key. We can easily look at larger ministries and think, *If only I had their resources, things would be different for me.* This thinking is a paralyzing trap that does not warrant belief. Bigger does not always equal better. What we can know is that God has equipped us to do His work where He has planted us. We are charged with making the best use of our time and resources, to be good stewards in maximizing the opportunities that He has given us.

Anyone can make a difference anywhere and can have a successful, impactful ministry. However, we must understand that ministry is hard work. A successful ministry takes a calling, motivation, persistence, resolve, sweat, tears, prayer, passion, the capacity to love, and the desire to serve and make a difference. The purpose of this book is to provide a systematic approach to help our life's mission of service be the very best that it can be for Christ. Let's journey together and see what God has in store for us.

—Daniel C. Morris
Summer 2015

Introduction

No one told us that we would have to be an administrator, politician, financial genius, servant, psychologist, producer, graphic designer, sound technician, media expert, Bible scholar, disciplinarian, trainer, and teacher—all while having a great personality. Worship pastors wear many hats in their unique roles. Other than the pastor, it is one of the few ministry positions in the church that is constantly in the public eye, as well as in the throes of everyday ministry to the entire church family. How do we accomplish these dual roles well with maximum impact and still continue to grow the kingdom of God?

Many worship pastors, young and older, struggle to do the basics of ministry and spend years just figuring out how to survive another week, with little to no lasting impact on their congregations or music participants. With most churches in America averaging seventy to eighty in worship attendance, practical resources can be hard to come by or nonexistent. Even worship pastors in churches of significant size often struggle to move their ministry forward beyond congregational or special music singing.

Moving beyond this basic ministry level is how I want to help others. I do not have all the answers (and never will), but I have been that guy who tried to make sense of it all and did the very best I could to survive. I have walked the road of inexperience and nonexposure—not knowing what I did not know. While I have had a few mentors along the way, they were neither plentiful nor beat down my door to give me helpful advice. Some may disagree with me, but in my experience, ministers of music do not talk to one another very productively. Some may; most do not. It may be that we do not know how to articulate the nuances of ministry, or perhaps it is the insecurity and vulnerability that come from exposing our failures and successes to one another.

I recently surveyed several of my colleagues and discussed this idea of silence among our counterparts. All except one agreed that in their experience, worship leaders do not provide much "sharing" when it comes to success in music and worship ministry. Several responded that they felt it was because of insecurity—not wanting to see others succeed. Most said that everything they have learned outside the classroom was learned by trial and a lot of error. Except for my ministry education and the occasional worship conference, I have had to learn on my own. I learned by doing and watching others. I learned by listening to and by obeying, as best as I knew how, the leadership of the Holy Spirit. And of course, I too learned through trial and error.

In order to take the first step toward success, we have to realize that there is more that can be done for the cause of Christ than hovering at the very basic level. Second, we have to come to the place where we recognize that we are not living up to our potential or to God's standards when it comes to His kingdom. Third, we must be willing to take the steps necessary to accomplish God's plan for our ministry.

Let me provide a snapshot of my background. I grew up in a small rural Southern Baptist Church. My father was a volunteer music leader, and my mother was the pianist. *The Broadman Hymnal* was the only music book that our congregation sang from until we were able to update to the 1975 *Baptist Hymnal*. Worship planning was easy: just fill in the hymn numbers in the bulletin's order of service, give a copy to my mother, and bingo, service planning is done—and all before the Sunday school bell rings. It was not until I graduated from high school, moved away from home, and began attending a larger church with a music ministry program that I was exposed to multifaceted, age-graded music and worship ministry. My experience and perspective were limited.

After surrendering to full-time church music ministry, I began pursuing my church music degree. Not until then was I exposed to a world of possibilities and ideas for music ministry. I was thrilled and eager to put to use what I was learning.

Soon God gave me that opportunity, and I realized quickly that I was clueless. I knew nothing. Even though I was inexperienced and ignorant, I was a go-getter. I made the decision that I could just figure things out. By having the opportunity to serve with a former large-church pastor, Dr. Ernest Bailey, the Lord gave me the chance to learn from him and be deepened in my perspective of ministry. Dr. Bailey challenged everything that I knew about music ministry and leadership. He spurred in me a desire to move forward, to change, and to think outside of myself. He inspired me to make a greater impact. The Lord used that time to teach me that there was something greater that He wanted me to do. I did not understand it at the time, but soon the Lord opened the door for me to make a ministry move to Westside Baptist Church in Gainesville, Florida.

Upon arriving at Westside, I quickly—within hours—found that I had stepped into an environment that was beyond my experience and exposure. "Fake it 'til you make it" was not going to work at Westside. There was a higher level of expectation and accountability. The environment at Westside was fast-paced and challenging. From the first day until this very day, nearly ten years later, every part of my ministry, my intentions, my integrity, my character, my skill, and my mind have been challenged to the core. Granted, I am the type of person who thrives and even enjoys that kind of environment. But I have made a discovery: many staff members do not have an appreciation for a higher level of accountability. Most seem to want the end result of challenge and hard work, but not everyone is willing to pay the price to achieve those end results. Tony Bridwell, author and partner with Partners In Leadership, says it this way: "There are two basic groups of people: the sitters and the getters. Most people think accountability is something bad, so they don't want it." Many would rather just work within the status quo of ministry, content not to be challenged, or to make a greater contribution to the work of the church, their community, or even their life.

The more I see this complacency in colleagues of mine, the more my heart breaks for the abundant life that is not experienced by those who have surrendered to a call of God in their life. Many are like who I used to be! They want to make a difference but just do not know how. For these seekers, I am writing this book. This information is for those who are just like who I was, for those who want to make a difference but do not know how, for those who want to move forward but do not know which direction to go.

I keep in mind that class is still in session for me, and I hope and pray that I am always the student. The more I learn, the more I realize that I do not know very much. This book will not answer all the questions or address all the challenges that we are facing or will face in ministry. But hopefully, it can serve as a starting point for moving us from where we are today to somewhere different, somewhere better. These are just ideas and principles that I have picked up along the way in my short journey. I hope maybe just one of them can help someone else.

SECTION 1

Starting Points for Success

Prayer — An Essential for Success

Prayer is the most often talked about,
but the least practiced discipline in the Christian life.

—Daniel Henderson[1]

LIKE MOST PEOPLE, when I get leadership and ministry help books, I arm myself with a highlighter and a pen to start skimming the chapters of the book, mining for those gold nuggets that I can apply to my ministry or teach to my team. Often I do not linger, especially when I think that I know where the author is going. I run this risk with my readers by starting a book with a chapter on prayer. Really, what could I possibly say about prayer that has not already been said? I imagine some will read the title of this chapter and think, *That's nice that he starts with prayer, kudos,* and then move through the chapter scanning for those nuggets.

Some readers may be in what seems to be the smallest church on the planet with no resources whatsoever, except a dream, a

---

1 Daniel Henderson, *Fresh Encounters: Experiencing Transformation through United Worship-Based Prayer* (Colorado Springs, CO: NavPress, 2008), 24.

willingness to serve, and maybe seven to ten singers interested in forming a small choir. Some others may be seasoned ministers of music in an urban church with a 250-member choir and orchestra, with specialized staff and with multifaceted ministry components. Anywhere on this spectrum of ministry, from the smallest of the small to the largest of mega or somewhere in between, this chapter could make the greatest difference. It is not what I write about prayer that is going to make an impression; it will be the act of praying and the results of prayer that will bring blessings and could revolutionize our ministries. Prayer will affect every detail of the way the Christian leader leads.

To each of us, prayer means something different. We have seen prayer work in many varied ways. But there is a huge difference between saying prayers and praying! "Prayer is not a preface or an addition to the work of the ministry; it is the work of ministry."[2]

I am a *builder*. God has equipped my brain to think of how I can take something small and maximize its potential. I used to think that the best goal in ministry would be to build an organization from small to big (or as big as possible) and then move on. I staked my significance as a leader on the ability to grow a ministry. This philosophy may have some merit, but it is not God's biblical standard. It was my standard. Through tears and struggling constantly to gain significance by continually growing, the Lord finally and gently delivered me from that way of thinking. Building an organizational giant should not be the goal or the source of my significance; making a difference for eternity should be. Eternal significance is the ultimate vision of a successful ministry.

---

2   Quote adapted from Oswald Chambers's original quote: "Prayer does not fit us for the greater work; prayer is the greater work." Source unknown.

Any leader, no matter how big or how small the ministry, can make an impact for eternity. I used to think that if I could only have a bigger budget and more people to influence, then I could make a greater impact for Christ. In theory, this thinking may seem like a great argument. But we all know those right now who have as many resources as they could possibly hope for, with people surrounding them, but they have no idea or concept of making a significant kingdom impact. Prayer is the difference maker! Prayer is the dividing line and is pivotal in sustaining the life of a believer and the effectiveness of ministry. Jesus says to us, "But seek first his kingdom and his righteousness, and all these things will be given to you as well" (Matthew 6:33, NIV)

Let's face it, we do not always feel like praying. Sometimes the words are just not there. This is why it is so important to develop a discipline of authentic, biblically based prayer.

J. Oswald Sanders identifies with this difficulty of developing the lifestyle of prayer: "True prayer is a strenuous spiritual exercise that demands the utmost mental discipline and concentration."[3]

"Prayer begins with and is fueled by God and His character, not our needs."[4] Prayer that is controlled by the Holy Spirit will reflect the heart of God Himself. It will be void of the usual wants and requests for shallow personal desires but be full of praise and the essence of His nature. Andrew Murray says, "Some people pray just to pray and some people pray to know God."[5] Once we realize the power that comes from a life of genuine prayer, then we begin to view prayer differently.

---

3   J. Oswald Sanders, *Spiritual Leadership: Principles of Excellence for Every Believer*, [Updated ed. (Chicago, IL: Moody Publishers, 2007), 86.

4   Andrew Murray, *With Christ in the School of Prayer*, Barbour Publishing, 1981.

5   Murray, *With Christ in the School of Prayer*.

Prayer is the means by which we can grow in our faith, life, and ministry. Without prayer, we are powerless to face the enemy Satan and to face the circumstances where we may find ourselves. "When you work, you work; when you pray, God works."[6] When I need a fresh wind from the Lord, I pray. When I need balance in my life between ministry and home, I pray. When I need someone to talk to and no one else will understand, I pray. When I have a victory in ministry, I pray. Do you see the pattern? Philippians 4:6 says, "Do not be anxious about anything, but in everything, by prayer and petition, with thanksgiving, present your requests to God."

We can all remember those moments when we have prayed for the latest new techno gadget that we were sure was "completely necessary" for ministry, or some of us may have prayed that the old hymnals would spontaneously combust. We have all prayed for things that we do not need and things that do not necessarily reflect the heart of God. Some people think that it is wrong to ask God for things. I believe that God not only wants us to ask, but He wants to give us the desires of our hearts (Psalm 37:4). However, we must rely on the Holy Spirit to guide us in the things that we desire and should ask for them in prayer. This reliance comes from spending time in prayer with Him. John 14:13–14 says, "And I will do whatever you ask in my name, so that the Son may bring glory to the Father. You may ask me for anything in my name, and I will do it."

Sometimes we question, Should I even ask for growth in my ministry? The answer is, of course!

In my early days at Westside, we were growing an instrumental ministry. We had a basic rhythm section already and a few sparse instruments (a flute, a violin, and a trumpet). I told my

6   Max Lucado, *Turn: Remembering Our Foundations* (Sisters, OR: Multnomah Books, 2005).

ministry assistant that I wanted to pray that God would grow the instrumental ministry to fifteen players within the next six months. We would need to add eight players. She looked at me as if I were crazy, and I sometimes thought so too. But we began to pray. We prayed specifically for the instruments that we desired. God delivered on time. I cannot explain what happened any other way. The players just came. Sometime later, we needed to build our brass section with some lower brass instruments. We prayed again, and God delivered. Then woodwinds, we prayed specifically for woodwinds, and God brought us woodwinds. We did not have any other explanation other than prayer.

Someone recently asked me how I grew our instrumental ministry, what strategy I used. I looked at him, smiled, and said, "Friend, I am sorry that I do not have a more complicated answer for you than this: we just prayed, and God gave us the people." He was blown away by my response, and to be honest, so was I, but also humbled. When I think about what has happened, I realize that every season of growth in our ministry has been the result of prayer. We have been very specific in our prayers over the years.

Prayer can change a situation, and if it does not change the circumstances, it can change the way we see them. In his book *Fresh Encounters*, Daniel Henderson writes,

> Prayer transcends our best effort to grow a church or build a ministry. The church is not a corporation but a community of people. It is not an organization, but an organism. It is not an enterprise for Christ but an experience of Christ. It is supernatural and can only meet His standards through supernatural means. Because of that, prayer is indispensable.[7]

---

7   Daniel Henderson, *Fresh Encounters*, 70.

Whether we are a volunteer minister with a pianist who can only read what is on the page of the hymnal, or we are trying to get a fledgling ministry off the ground, or we are in a megachurch leading a large ministry with the ability to perform the most extremely orchestrated pieces of music—our best effort for success in kingdom impact may not be to add to the numbers, but it may be to add a new dimension of spiritual depth through prayer.

> Always respond to every impulse to pray. The impulse to pray may come when you are reading or when you are battling with a text. I would make an absolute law of this—always obey such an impulse. (Martyn Lloyd-Jones)[8]

Questions for Reflection

1. Is my prayer life with God intimate and constant?
2. Do I spend more time asking God to bless me, or do I use prayer to worship and listen to God speak?
3. Do I really desire to know God more deeply through prayer?
4. Am I afraid to ask God for growth and challenge in my life and ministry?

Next Steps for Success

1. Pray asking God to deepen your prayer life with Him.
2. Establish a consistent time to be in prayer.
3. Schedule strategic times of prayer on your calendar in order to make prayer a focus of your life and ministry.

---

8   Martyn Lloyd-Jones, *Preaching and Preachers*, (Grand Rapids, MI: Zondervan, 1971), 170.

2

Worship Every Day

I will praise you as long as I live, and in
your name I will lift up my hands.

—Psalm 63:4 (NIV)

"OUR INSTINCTIVE RESPONSE in knowing God personally is worship. And worship is His strategic plan for all of creation."[1] God provided a framework in His Word by which we can worship within a lifestyle of relationship with Him. The word *relationship* includes the idea of a lifestyle, not just a scheduled exercise. In other words, the true worship of God is not limited to our regular church attendance. The worship of God is demonstrated by how we live our lives and conduct ourselves under the influence and ultimate control of the Holy Spirit. The Holy Spirit of God is the indicator of the presence of God in our lives. God chose to send the Holy Spirit to dwell within and among us so that we can know Him and His ways. God certainly went out of His way to ensure that we can be in relationship with Him. "Without His

---

1   Vernon Whaley, *Called to Worship: the Biblical Foundations of Our Response to God's Call*, reprinted (Nashville: Thomas Nelson, 2013), 3.

presence we will not worship, but when God is with us, when He is present, worship is our immediate response."[2]

We all worship something. By God's design, every human being was created with the need to worship. Because God created us for worship, the worship of God is the foundation of a life of faith in Christ. Surprisingly enough, we spend a lot more time unengaged in the worship of our Creator simply because we have placed other things in the way. For many of us, the act of worship can become the object of our praise; the songs, the sets, the feeling of the congregation singing and responding. All these things are elements of worship that can easily become what we long for. Worship leaders can lead music during corporate worship times and fail to worship the Lord personally.

Unfortunately, I hate to admit that I have done this many times myself. My proclivity is to define my Sunday success by how smooth everything goes and how well we execute our planning. For me, it certainly takes discipline and focus to manage a large music ministry program on Sunday mornings: execute sound checks; warm up the choir, orchestra, and praise team; lead three worship services that are all time sensitive while working with additional simultaneous venues that are dependent on my hitting my mark. But it takes even more discipline, intentionality, and focus for me to do all these things and worship God too. Let me stop and say that this is not a challenge that just started for me when I stepped into a larger ministry environment. This challenge was also present when I led a smaller music program. Our capacity to manage all the details and truly engage in worship will always be a challenge. That is why it is so important that the weekend service is not our only worship experience. That is not God's plan for us.

---

2   Ibid., 6.

When we approach a Sunday worship experience, it is essential that we have adequately prepared spiritually and have been worshiping personally every day. Our corporate worship experiences should be the overflow of our private time with the Lord, not our Sunday routine.

What does it mean to worship every day? It means living our lives in a manner that brings honor to God and is faithful and obedient to Him in every way. We may ask, In what way is "every" way? The answer is, *every* way! What we say, wear, watch, drive, the music we listen to, who our friends are, how we act in the office, our disposition, how much we tip after a meal out, what we text, post on social media, and yes, even how we respond to the employee in the drive-through who got our order wrong—twice. Absolutely everything under the sun should be considered in the light of how it brings glory and honor to our Creator. Thinking like this can completely revolutionize our world and actually bring some unintended sinful practices to light. Can we live a perfect lifestyle of worship this side of heaven? No, but we can consistently live lives that are in relationship with God and are controlled by the Holy Spirit. When we are in a growing worship relationship with God, we will find that suddenly ungodliness around us becomes a huge turnoff. We will want to flee from the things that grieve the Holy Spirit and interrupt our worship relationship. What are practical ways to help us live a lifestyle of worship every day?

Personal Times of Worship

Personal worship times are critical moments when we can worship and focus on the Lord. We must build time into each day for opportunities to think and meditate on the Lord. I am not talking about a daily quiet time. Remember those? I am talking about moving beyond the onetime morning moment with the Lord to a continual interaction of prayer and worship throughout the day. We can turn off the radio or CD player while driving and spend time thinking about the blessings and goodness of the Lord. We can sing out loud to Him. Strategically placed scripture on index cards around the house or the office can help fuel a relationship with the Lord and help us continually think about Him and His Word. These days, it is easy to set up scripture quotations and reflective devotional thoughts to pop up on our smartphones.

Just like a relationship with our spouse, our kids, or our friends, we continually and intentionally have to nurture our relationship with the Lord. It is rare that we would talk only once a day to our immediate family members or friends. Instead, we constantly interact with the people whom we love and desire to have a relationship with. This same concept should be present when growing our relationship with God. Just as we have to put forth an effort to develop our earthly relationships, we also have to look intentionally for creative ways to develop our worship relationship with God.

Living a Life of Excellence

Worship is expressed in the life of believers when our lives give glory to God. This happens when we live life with excellence. "Whatever you do, work at it with all your heart, as working for the Lord, not for human masters, since you know that you will receive an inheritance from the Lord as a reward. It is the Lord Christ you are serving."[3] We need to set a standard of excellence for ourselves and then lead others to do the same. Working with excellence and leading others to minister with excellence are acts of worship. Life does not live itself. We have to work at it, make decisions, and respond to circumstances. Either we

---

3   Colossians 3:23–24 (NIV)

respond poorly, make bad decisions, and live life haphazardly—or we plan, respond to life with wisdom and courage, and make good decisions.

Growing as a person, learning new things, and generally seeking to improve so that we can be better in life and ministry are all acts of worship. Being an encouragement and building relationships with the people around us is an act of worship. In his book *The Pursuit of Excellence*, Ted Engstrom says, "The highest and best—this should be the goal of every man and woman of God."[4] This pattern of living a life of excellence must be present in the life of a leader, who is making strides toward moving from survival to success personally and in ministry. But beware, every truly worthwhile achievement of excellence has a price tag. Contrary to popular belief, success is not handed to us. Unfortunately, even the well-meaning Christian who lives a God-fearing life is not necessarily guaranteed success. A dynamic life does not come with ease or by chance. Influence does not come automatically or because of personality. Sacrifice, long days, short nights, hard work, pain, heartache, failure, blood, sweat, and tears are required for a life and ministry of depth, vitality, influence, and excellence. We all must answer the question, How much are we willing to pay in sacrifice, patience, endurance, and hard work to be a person of excellence? Our answer is important because the cost is great.

Excellence does not mean perfection. There is only one person who was ever perfect, and that is Jesus Christ. However, excellence is still apparent and present even in our failures and struggles. We can worship God when we respond to life's challenges, failures, and successes with the excellent and holy nature of Christ. When we think of living a lifestyle of worship, the quality of our job performance, the thoughtful choices that we make, how organ-

---

4   Ted W. Engstrom, *The Pursuit of Excellence* (Grand Rapids, MI: Zondervan Publishing Company, 1982), 18.

ized we are, and how detailed our plans—these may not be the first things to cross our minds. Nevertheless, living this kind of life and ministry is an act of worship that demonstrates the love of Christ through us.

Sharing Our Faith with Others

Obedience in personal evangelism is a distinct way that we can worship the Lord every day. A relationship with God fans the flames of Great Commission worship. "Generations of anemic worship have resulted in an impotent faith that reduces worship to an act of personal expression and ignores Jesus' command to share the gospel."[5] Looking and praying for opportunities to share Christ with our family members, friends, neighbors, and coworkers will be a natural outflow of worship.

Can I just say this to my worship leader friends? Neither our weekly platform ministry nor our Christmas and Easter programs take the place of personal and intentional evangelism. Although we lead a potentially very evangelistic ministry within the church body, it would be foolish for us to think that our Great Commission task is complete. I seriously doubt that any of us would hold our pastors to that standard. Why should we think that would be all right for us? Our ministry positions are administratively heavy and require a lot of time at the office. We are engaged in many areas of ministry organization and leading and training people. This kind of schedule makes it very difficult to engage in intentional evangelism outside of our ministry endeavors. There is, however, this crazy thing that happens when we are worshiping the Lord every day and spending time with Him. We will be compelled to share our faith with others. There

---

5   David Wheeler and Vernon M. Whaley, *Worship and Witness: Becoming a Great Commission Worshiper* (Nashville: LifeWay Press, 2013) 161.

seems to be this sense of unrest and conviction that comes to a growing believer who is in a worship relationship with God.

This practice of worshiping every day will bring a distinct difference in our outlook and management of life, family, and leadership. Rehearsals will be different, and leadership of the church family on Sunday mornings will be different. Certainly, the church family will notice. After we make steps toward success in our own life and ministry, our next step is to lead others, teaching them what we are learning. When the Lord is at work in our lives and teaching us new things, we can begin to seek ways to share those experiences with those we lead. We can tell them about our journey and challenge the church family, and especially participants in our ministry, in this area of everyday worship. We can create a leadership lesson and introduce it to our praise team. If that goes well, we can teach the concepts to our music leadership team and to the choir and orchestra. After a while of teaching our people about worshiping every day, what that means, and practical ways they can accomplish that goal, they will begin to tell us their stories. In our ministry, people even made a hashtag: #worshipeveryday. As their daily worship began to change, they became freer and more expressive in corporate worship times. Our weekend services have become an overflow of what has happened all week.

We have worked to build a culture where our people are thinking about worship every day, but it all starts with us. If we are not worshiping every day, we will not be able to experience the fullness that God desires for us. The depth and power of a corporate worship time can be traced back to the prayer and worship that is happening in the personal lives of the ones leading. In a Passion Conference in 1997, Beth Moore said something that I have never forgotten. She said, "You show me someone with a stale ministry, and I'll show you someone who has lost intimacy with God." Success and significance in ministry start with a life that worships God fresh and new every day.

Questions for Reflection

1. Is my worship pervasive in my life, or is it just reserved for my Sunday worship service?
2. Have I developed the discipline of a daily quiet time? If no, why not?
3. Do I seek to live a life of excellence in every way?
4. How long has it been since I have shared the Gospel with someone who does not know Christ?

Next Steps for Success

1. Establish a regular meeting time with the Lord and ask someone to hold you accountable for this time.
2. Make a list of the areas in your life that you want to improve. Develop a process to raise the standard of these areas.
3. Make a list of lost people whom you know. Begin praying for them and ask the Lord for an opportunity to share with them.
4. Take your Bible and highlight scripture that could be easily identified and used when sharing the Gospel with someone.

3

Time in the Word of God

For the word of God is living and active.
sharper than any double-edged sword,
it penetrates even to dividing soul and
spirit, joints and marrow;
it judges the thoughts and attitudes of the heart.

—Hebrews 4:12 (NIV)

EVEN AS A believer, it was years before I realized the definitive impact that the Word of God could have on my life and ministry. It is true that God reveals His Word to us as we are able to understand it, and the more we read, the more we will want to read. When we commit to this process, the Word of God begins to shape and change our actions, thoughts, and decision-making processes. Our leadership capacity will be increased by the time spent reading God's Word and understanding its principles. As leaders, we need to take a look at our perspective and leadership as it relates to the Word of God. "Spiritual leaders of every generation will have a consuming passion to know the Word of God through diligent study and the illumination of the Holy

Spirit."[1] Are we allowing the Word of God to penetrate and permeate our thinking and our everyday activities? If not, we can begin by praying that the Lord reveal His Word to us; then we can get help in understanding through commentaries, devotional insights, and other parallel readings.

Time in the Word of God will need to move to the top of our daily priorities if it is not there already. For those of us who are in survival mode, this may seem like a *huge* undertaking. It is unrealistic to think that we might go from spending very little time in the Word on a daily basis to making it a top daily priority overnight. I have found that if we begin to take small steps of exposure to the Word of God, our appetite will grow; and before we know it, we will have an unsatisfied hunger. There are a few things that I have found works for me when needing to increase my success in this area.

One of the ways that we can quickly increase our time spent in the Word of God is to teach it. Let's ask ourselves these kinds of questions: With what group could I currently lead a Bible study? What about leading a Bible study with my praise team or with the choir and orchestra? Right now, I am leading a Bible study with the music and media staff, as well as the praise team. Last summer, I taught a Bible study on worship that was open to the whole church. Teaching this class on worship proved to be a great blessing to me and drew me closer to the Lord. Teaching forces us to cultivate the habit of getting into the Word of God.

During corporate worship times, we can use quotations or ideas from these Bible studies and incorporate them into what we are doing. This practice accomplishes at least two things: First, it creates an intentional teaching time for the whole congregation. Second, it makes a connection and reinforces the concepts to

---

1   J. Oswald Sanders, *Spiritual Leadership: Principles of Excellence for Every Believer*, [Updated ed. (Chicago, IL: Moody Publishers, 2007), 102.

the persons who are taking the Bible study class. As we watch the students in our class begin to apply the biblical teachings in their corporate worship, we can see how the Lord has changed them in their biblical expression and attitude toward worship. I cannot adequately express how I have seen the difference that this teaching experience has made in a large part of our congregation.

Sometimes, especially in small ministries, we may think that we do not have influence over many people and that teaching a Bible study class would not have much influence on the entire congregation. Think about this challenge: What if we were to teach a Bible study class on worship to twenty choir members? What if, during the class, ten of those people were equipped to teach or share what they have learned? Those ten people may have influence over ten more. Now our influence has multiplied, and the things that we have been teaching from the scripture to only a few now have the potential to influence many others. Does this sound familiar? Jesus invested in the lives of twelve men who changed the world forever. We do not have to have scores of people to teach; Jesus had twelve. We may have only four or five. Whatever God has entrusted to us, we need to make the most of it.

Another way to increase our Bible study is to take a higher education class that requires reading and Bible study. We can never learn too much. While these classes can be expensive, we will certainly benefit from what we learn.

Whatever method we choose or what our motivation is to get started with Bible study, the most important thing is to get started. We will never regret getting into God's Word. And the great truth is that the more we know, the more we will want to know.

Knowing the Word of God is to know and understand the will of God. Sometimes we say, "I am trying to understand the will of God." We need to realize that God's will is not a secret. He has revealed His will for our lives in His Word. He has even revealed His will for our ministry in the pages of scripture. If we want to know what our next step in ministry should be, we have a silver bullet: increased prayer and intentionality with the Word of God. He is ready to speak to us. The Holy Spirit is active and at work in guiding the lives of believers who are in communication with God through the Bible and prayer.

Here are a few practical and simple ways that we can help ourselves be under the constant influence of the Word of God:

1. Write out scripture on index cards. We can keep a stack of scripture cards on our desks and/or carry them in our pockets.
2. Use sticky notes to write out scripture. We can place these notes in strategic places where we will see them often, such as the bathroom mirror, the refrigerator, the kitchen counter, a window, or at the bottom of the computer screen. We can keep them on the dashboard of our car (or truck) so that we can meditate on scripture while driving.
3. Reinforce scripture through music. We can go through our music library and make a playlist of worship songs whose lyrics are scripture. Bible verses set to music provide a great way to learn scripture.
4. Get creative with technology. This generation spends a great amount of time with mobile technology. We can put one of the many Bible apps on our smartphone or tablet.

The result of consistent times of prayer and Bible study is a life controlled by the Holy Spirit. We often neglect the Holy Spirit or think of the work of the Holy Spirit as an occasional visitation into our lives. But this thinking is not true today, nor was it true throughout the Bible. Scripture says that the Holy Spirit indwells the people of God and prompts the believer in everyday matters. The Holy Spirit seeks to control our thoughts, speech, and planning. This control can only be realized through understanding the character of God through time in His Word.

We can challenge ourselves to begin now to pray for a fresh encounter with the Word of God. We must ask the Lord to give us the desire and the ability to study and understand what He is saying to us through the Bible.

Questions for Reflection

1. With what group could I currently lead a Bible study?
2. Have I made excuses for not learning and memorizing scripture?
3. Do I spend time consistently in the Word of God?

Next Steps for Success

1. Identify a topic or scripture to be possibly used for a Bible study. Set a date to start.
2. Develop a process to help you memorize scripture. Ask someone to help you.
3. Schedule strategic times of Bible study. When choosing passages to read, be intentional and systematic, as well as open to the prompting of the Holy Spirit.

Success with Family

For if anyone does not know how to
manage his own household,
how can he take care of God's church.

—1 Timothy 3:5 (NIV)

SECOND ONLY TO God and His call on my life must be my family. My family has to be a top priority and more important than any rehearsal or ministry meeting. I need to be willing to walk off the platform at any time for the sake of my family. They are a gift and a treasure from the Lord. I do not want my wife or children ever to question my love and devotion to them. Even though there are ministry seasons, such as Christmas and Easter, that demand much attention, I try hard to make sure that my family does not feel neglected on a continuing basis. Unfortunately, this standard has not always been true for me. There was a time when I did not understand how to keep family and ministry balanced.

I love what I do! Ministry is my passion. I am constantly thinking about ministry matters. There is nothing wrong with being passionate and in love with one's calling. But there was a time when I was not intentional about my schedule and my priorities. Therefore, my family, especially my wife, paid the price. Fortunately, I came to the realization that I could have a high-energy, growing, and successful ministry and also a great homelife. This balance is essential as we move to a higher level of leadership. We have to learn to lead ourselves well and develop an organized and systematic approach to ministry. Is this balance always perfect in our ministry and lives? No, of course not. There will always be certain seasons when the ministry demand is heavy; those are the times for special precautions. This combination of high-energy ministry and good family life is never easy; at times it is super hard. With the help of our family members, we have to get creative in figuring how to make family life work.

While there are times when life can become unbalanced, one thing is clear: we cannot become an absent parent at home. With good communication, careful planning, and strong leadership, we can have both a great family life and a successful ministry.

Here are a few practices that my wife and I have put into place to help our family face the rigors of ministry.

Prayer and Devotional Times

With our wild and crazy family, devotional times have been a challenge! However, we have always tried to do family prayer and/or devotional time. Right now, our two oldest children are six and three years old. Each night, we sit on the floor and read a Bible story and pray together. Everyone gets a turn to pray, even my three-year-old. He says the words he can say, and we guide him. He folds his hands like the rest of us. This time is so precious and rich for us because not only is it a family time, but my wife and I get to model prayer for our children. As our children grow, this model will change, but we are building a foundation for that future. For all of us—whether we have babies, young children, teenagers, or no children—we need to be in a habit of praying and reading God's Word together.

Family Fun Time

We now live about two hours from Disney World. My wife and I made a decision several years ago that we would forfeit gifts for each other so that we could afford annual passes to Disney World. This is our gift to each other and to our children, and we all love to go. Each trip is a gift and a memory maker for us.

It does not have to be Disney World; it can be trips to the beach, hiking, or whatever is available close by. Playing in the sprinklers in the front yard is one of the most enjoyable things we do! We just need to plan fun times with our families. These special shared moments will build lasting memories.

On the last trip we made, we were struggling with the arrangements, and the choices came down to the cost. My mother-in-law shared this insight with my wife: "A year from now you will not remember the cost. You will only remember what you did together." As long as we are spending within our means, we can make decisions based on memories. The point is that we need to do things that make memories.

Visits to the Office

It is always fun when the Morris clan comes to my office to visit. I love hearing my kids run down the hall and around the corner to barrel through the door. They get to see where I am when I am not with them. Having my kids visit the office occasionally helps me feel a greater connection with them during each day. Before we had kids, my wife would come to the office and clean or organize something.

I remember, as a kid, visiting my dad at his office. It was always an exciting time. A family gathering at the office (other than Sunday) is just another way that we can build strength and continuity between our ministry and the family dynamic.

Participation in Ministry

For my family, this involvement is a given; for some, circumstances may make this more difficult. My wife sings on our worship team and in the choir. She is the backstage coordinator for our Christmas production, as well as an artistic director. She is also a very gifted teacher and communicator and has her own areas of ministry outside of the music ministry.

Ministry together is sometimes difficult, especially with the kids, but the effort is worthwhile because we get to see each other more often. During the Christmas preparation season, there are weeks when I am at the church every night. If it were not for her participation in the production, we would not see very much of each other during this time. Also, my wife has been the source of many of my good ideas in ministry. She often has very creative ideas for songs, service elements, and ministry programming.

All wives may not be able to participate as mine can. Spouses with jobs outside the home may have a special challenge with limited time for ministry. And not all spouses want to be involved in music. However, there may be something at sometime that allows a spouse to be involved and connected. There are always needs for volunteers in the office or for organizing files. We need to be creative and look for ways for these connections. The point is to be intentional in finding something, anything that can be shared together in ministry.

Date Night

Finding time for date night is one of the most difficult challenges that my wife and I face right now. We have three young children, one still in diapers. Date night is hard to make a reality, but we know that it is desperately needed. We value this principle and have date night as often as possible.

Some couples have date night regularly, and I say bravo and aspire to achieve this goal. Date night is a critical and necessary experience for spouses. This special time together can help foster intimacy and rejuvenation from the strains of ministry life. We must be intentional to make date night happen.

I try to have a systematic approach to spending a balanced time with family. Here is the suggestion:

- Once per week = something special (game night, out-to-eat night, etc.)
- Once per month = date night (a special time for mom and dad)
- Once per quarter = special fun weekend/special activity, event
- Once per year = family vacation/significant getaway

Family is so important. We must cherish our families. We should be willing to make changes in our schedule to make sure that our families are not being neglected. And as our family dynamic changes, we must reevaluate our needs and make necessary adjustments to meet those needs. Remember that it is not the extravagance and monetary value that will make the difference; it is the quality time that our families will remember. We can make a wonderful memory without spending a dime. However, when planning our budgets, we should not think of family time as a frivolous spending category. It can actually be an investment with the greatest return!

Success as a Single Adult

"Christianity's founder, Jesus Christ, and leading theologian, St. Paul were both single their entire lives."[1] There have been significant contributions to the kingdom of God made by single men and women. Right now, at Westside, we have several single adults serving on our staff. I want to take a moment to speak to those who are single and working to be successful in ministry. Single adults have a profound opportunity to serve the Lord with full attention on the needs of the people being served, as well as putting full thought to the organizational needs of building a successful and impactful ministry.

Practice Discipline

I encourage single adults to dig deep in self-leadership and discipline. Establish healthy habits in life and ministry now that will be good preparation for a future family and ministry. Become spiritually disciplined in prayer and seek a deepened relationship with the Lord. A scripture that was profound for me before I was married and was young in ministry was 1 Timothy 4:12: "Don't let anyone look down on you because you are young, but set an example for believers in life, in love, in faith, and in purity."

Be Smart with Finances

When I was young and single, I did not think about what I needed to do with my money to be in the best possible position for my future. I did not think about investments, nor did I consider my retirement plan. This oversight is one of my regrets as a young

---

1   Timothy J. Keller and Kathy Keller, *The Meaning of Marriage: Facing the Complexities of Commitment with the Wisdom of God* (New York: Riverhead Books, 2013), 222.

minister. We cannot buy back time. As early as we can, all of us should be making wise choices with our finances to help create a successful future. For the single staff members who have come through our ministry, I have strongly encouraged them to go ahead and start planning for retirement, investments, and legacy.

Do Not Be Afraid to Date

We have become afraid of the word *date*. First of all, mentally processing the fact of feeling an attraction for someone is intense and emotional. Second, it is easy to become oversensitive to the opinions of others about whom and how we should have a relationship and how fast or slow that relationship should be moving. Both of these concerns are real and can be scary, but they should not create a fear that keeps a minister from obeying the Lord when it comes to dating. Here are a few thoughts when dating as a single minister:

1. Date with the intention of the possibility of marriage.
2. Date only a believer of like faith who has been called to a ministry of service.
3. Ask a few mature and unbiased friends to hold you accountable.
4. Accept the fact that people will have opinions. Date anyway.
5. Never be in a compromising position where integrity or purity can be questioned. Always be above reproach.
6. Let the relationship move at the appropriate pace.
7. Seek the guidance of the Holy Spirit in all areas of the relationship.

Hang Out with the Right People

"You are the average of the five people you spend the most time with."[2] When working to build a successful ministry and reputation, we must choose carefully whom we spend most of our time with. The people we choose will either add value to or detract value from our life and ministry. We need to make sure we are choosing people who add value to our lives. If we want to be a better musician, we should be around great musicians. If we want to be a better leader, we can hang around good leaders. If we want to be successful, we need to surround ourselves with successful people.

My associate is in his midtwenties, single, and called to full-time vocational ministry. He is a gifted speaker, and he is sharp with administrative responsibilities. I have learned a lot from him over the two years that he has been my associate. As we work closely together, I have picked up some of his personality traits and habits, and he has picked up some of mine. Our vocabulary has become very synonymous, and we can work very quickly and efficiently together. Our work relationship adds value to both of us on a daily basis. I can safely say that much of the level of my success is determined by the influence of people like my associate and his contribution to my life and ministry.

Success After Kids

I cannot speak from experience on this season of life, but let me briefly share what I have observed. Children have a way of complicating a marriage and a ministry. During the years that we have children to raise, we have to make compromises and decisions to make our family a priority. However, it is unfortunate

---

2   Jim Rohn, source unknown.

when some parents become slaves to their children and wrap their entire identity in the life of their kids. Depending on the age of children and the ages between them, the raising-children phase of life can be one of the shortest phases. When the children move out, mom and dad can be aimlessly lost about what to do now. They may even ask, "Who is this person that I am married to?" Sometimes it takes hard work to rediscover life and ministry after kids. Many ministers, however, bury themselves in their ministry and spend much of the time gained back at the office. This approach leaves the spouse at home feeling neglected and unfamiliar with the new dynamic of a home without children.

Some extremely significant ministry can be accomplished after the years of raising children. Experiences and stories can be used as ministry tools for the people we are called to love and lead. This is not a time to neglect our families! Our churches need us to be strong and have strong marriages. We can engage in ministry and teach other parents what it means to serve the Lord and raise a family. Here are a few principles that lead to a successful ministry after the children have left.

Still Keep Family a Priority

Just because the children are grown does not mean we can neglect our spouses and become buried in ministry work. We can take some time to be intentional about growing spiritually deeper as an empty-nest couple.

Establish New Traditions

Some of the family traditions with the children can be continued, and some may not be possible to continue. We can start some new traditions with our spouse. We can continue or revive date night or go out of town for a week of vacation. We can become involved in a ministry together—maybe a Bible study for the choir, praise team, etc.

Get Busy Investing in a Legacy

Legacy is twofold: a financial legacy and a personal legacy. We need to be serious about investments and planning for retirement and for provisions after we are gone. We will never have more time than now. More importantly, we should be living a life of personal investment. We can mentally, emotionally, and physically invest in our children and family—and then in our ministries. The personal legacy we leave for our children and friends is far more important than any financial investment we leave for them.

Whatever stage of family life we are in, we have a God-given opportunity to make a successful kingdom impact with our families. We cannot overlook the mission that we have right in our own homes! God is honored and worshiped when we nurture our families and teach them to be more like Christ. "The brighter our light is at home, the farther it shines around the world."[3]

Questions for Reflection

1. Do you already have an established prayer and devotional time with your family?
2. Is your family strategically involved in your ministry on some level?
3. As a single adult, do you have accountability in place to help you establish the spiritual, physical, and financial disciplines?
4. As an empty nester, are you establishing new traditions and keeping your family a priority?

3 Johnny Hunt, sermon preached at the Pastor's Conference of the Southern Baptist Convention, Baltimore, MD. 2014.

Next Steps for Success

1. Make a list of ways that your family could be involved in your ministry. Suggest tasks that every member of your family can do to get them involved.

2. Establish a systematic plan for your family's fun and memory-making times. You may want to try the once-a-week/month/quarter/year plan or make a plan that works for you.

3. Write the names of the top-five people whom you spend the most time with. Determine if these people add value to you or detract value from you. Pray about the next steps to take with your relationships.

4. Make a plan for your legacy. Write down your dreams and wishes. Create a plan to help make these come true.

5

A Ministry of Integrity

For we are taking pains to do what is right
not only in the eyes of the Lord
but also in the eyes of men.

—2 Corinthians 8:21 (NIV)

"Do WHAT YOU say, *when* you say, *how* you say." I learned this statement when I came to Westside. It was framed and hanging in almost every office I entered. I got the clue right away that character and integrity are very important and critical to a successful ministry in this environment. "Anyone can say he has integrity, but action is the real indicator of character."[1]

"There is no such thing as a minor lapse in integrity."[2] This connection between integrity and ministry is a simple concept that many people have trouble grasping, but it is a foundational basis for a successful life and ministry. Do we want a good reputation

---

1   John C. Maxwell, *The 21 Indispensable Qualities of a Leader: Becoming the Person That People Will Want to Follow* (Nashville, TN: T. Nelson, 1999), 4.

2   Thomas J. Peters and Robert H., Jr. Waterman, *In Search of Excellence: Lessons from America's Best-Run Companies*, Reprint ed. (New York: HarperBusiness, 2006).

in the church and the community? Do we want people to treat us with respect and speak well of us? Of course, we all want this!

Often we hear colleagues complain about how they are talked about or how they lack receiving respect. If we listen and observe these fellow ministers, we will usually discover that they are missing in one of the areas of "doing what you say, when you say, how you say." The tricky part is that we cannot miss one aspect of this concept and still build a respectable reputation.

Think about this simple example. Suppose I tell a man in my ministry that I will copy a song for him on CD by Friday so that he can be prepared to sing on Sunday. Will it be sufficient if I miss just one of the criteria? What if I wait until Saturday to copy the song onto the CD? I did what I said I would do, and I did it how I said I would, I just did not do it when I said I would. So what are the consequences? The man has less time to rehearse and may be less prepared for Sunday than he normally would be. This simple example may not seem to have huge consequences, but "you can never separate a leader's character from his actions."[3] People will become less and less forgiving if we continually do not keep our word even with the small things. Make no mistake! Lacking in this practice of dependability is an issue of poor integrity.

Of course, we can all make mistakes from time to time and drop the ball. But remember, there are no minor lapses in integrity. We either have it, or we do not. So what happens when we realize that we will not be able to do what we say, when we say, how we say? We should notify the person or group whose expectations we will be unable to meet or hold on to our agreement. This simple communication can allow us and the other people involved to come up with a suitable solution.

---

3   Maxwell, *The 21 Indispensable Qualities of a Leader: Becoming the Person That People Will Want to Follow. 4.*

Look at this matter from the other side. How many times have people we were depending on not followed through with a deadline or commitment? And how often have they just decided not to say anything at all? Immediately, we begin to try to understand why this person missed the deadline. In the end, there is always a loss of trust if the person has not communicated a reason in advance. Even a simple "I forgot" erodes a sliver of trust that must be earned again.

Power and Integrity on the Platform

What does "power and integrity on the platform" mean? It means having the power of the Holy Spirit working in and through the spiritually and mentally prepared people who are on the platform. It does not mean that everyone leading is perfect and flawless. But there is something unique and powerful about having a group of people who are in a dynamic and growing relationship with the Lord leading onstage. The only way to ensure this power completely is for us to spend time in prayer and in the Word of God through the week. One of the most dangerous setbacks for a public platform ministry is a lack of integrity spiritually and practically.

People watch what we do and listen to what we say. If these two things do not match up, a flaw in character is revealed. When this dissonance occurs, there is an immediate diminishing of platform integrity. Our integrity is built on the choices that we make every day, choices that shape our character. If we are guilty of making unwise choices in our ministry or our personal life, and we want to move toward a more impactful platform ministry, then we must begin today to manage our life and choices better.

Here are a few simple ways that can be helpful in gaining and maintaining personal integrity.

Staying Grounded in the Word of God and Prayer

This admonition seems very simple, but it is the most important thing we can do. When personal and ministry integrity are lacking, certainly spiritual vitality will also be lacking. If we spend time in the Word of God and in prayer with Him on a regular basis, then the Holy Spirit will control our words and actions.

Keeping Accountability

We need to find trusted people in our life who can keep us accountable. We must ask them to speak the truth into our life even if it makes us uncomfortable. We can develop a list of questions that they can ask us every week, questions that we must answer honestly.

Keeping Good Company

We are very likely to pick up the habits of the people whom we spend the most time with. We need to seek out people who have great reputations and visible lives of integrity. We will benefit from getting to know them and spending time with them. We can be honest and let them know that we are seeking to learn how to maintain a successful lifestyle of integrity. We can ask for their help and seek to learn from the way they act and the intentional choices that they make.

Staying Humble

"Humility is not thinking less of yourself, but thinking of yourself less."[4] Often we think that we have the right combination of

---

4   C.S. Lewis, *Mere Christianity: a Revised and Amplified Edition, with a New Introduction, of the Three Books, Broadcast Talks, Christian Behaviour, and Beyond Personality* (San Francisco: HarperOne, 2015).

words or that we have the best singing voice and, therefore, the Lord needs us to help Him! This kind of thinking is simply not true. When we realize that we are complete failures without the working of the Holy Spirit in our lives, then we have a chance of seeing power in our ministries.

Not only does our integrity affect our power on the platform, but so does the integrity of anyone else who shares the stage with us. If we have a praise team or orchestra member or staff person with a lifestyle of habitual sin, that lack of integrity can be a distraction to those we are trying to lead and greatly diminish our platform ministry. There may be occasions when we will have to ask one of our team members to step back from leadership so that he or she can get life's circumstances in order.

Over the years, I have found this policy to be good practice and one that protects the integrity of our platform ministry. So that we do not have to manage these issues on a one-on-one basis, we can develop a policy and covenant for anyone who serves on the platform as soloist, orchestra member, band member, or as part of the praise team. In these policies, we can spell out the expectations for godly living and provide support from scripture. When enlisting those who will lead on the platform, we can read these policies together and then give them the option of taking time to pray over the expectations. When we have a copy of this signed form on file and have to deal with an integrity issue, we can approach the conversation from a policy perspective. We can remind the person about the covenant he or she made to abstain from certain practices that could reflect poorly on our ministry together. With this reminder and a plan of restoration in place, we should be better able to handle these situations without getting emotions involved. It is more likely that most people will respond well and that our personal relationship with the person will survive. With this process, we are not personally pointing out flaws in character, the Bible is—the covenant and policy are the ones holding him or her accountable.

A very common situation that ministers of music face is handling persons who are not invested in the overall music ministry but who still want to sing a solo on Sunday mornings. Sometimes we are tempted to allow these persons to sing with the hope that this opportunity will get them interested and involved. Usually we do not see these persons again after their solo until around a major holiday when they appear again to gain their five minutes of platform time. Unfortunately, these people are usually just looking for a place to play or sing so that they can feel important. They do not show love or care for the music ministry or the people who faithfully serve every week. When these people take the stage, they rob our platform ministry of integrity. They do not glorify God or edify the body of Christ. Most of us have to deal with this issue every year. We can save ourselves time and frustration by developing a policy and procedure that protects our ministry and ourselves. If not, we become victims of these people, and our ministry is compromised and cheapened.

Here are some suggestions for policies that can be put into place to protect the integrity of our platform ministry:

1. Choir and orchestra members must be believers. There are churches with low standards that allow anyone who wants to sing to sing. We need to ask our ministry persons to share their salvation testimony before being considered a member of the choir or orchestra.
2. Music ministry members must regularly attend a Bible study class. People who are not plugged in and growing in their faith will not last in ministry. We need to check regularly the Bible study attendance of our choir and orchestra members.

3. Participants in all areas of the music ministry must be active members of the choir or orchestra. To sing a solo, sing in an ensemble, play in the handbell choir, or participate in any area of the music ministry, the person must first be an active member of the choir or orchestra.

When persons approach us about singing a solo, we can tell them that we have many opportunities for soloists and then tell them our process. Persons who are serious about being a member of the music ministry and serving the Lord gladly follow the process. Those who only want a gig never make it past the practiced policies. Following these simple procedures takes the guesswork out of our answers to people who threaten our platform integrity. These policies and processes not only protect our leadership, it also protects the people who serve in our ministry. They do not have to worry about sacrificing time to the ministry just to watch someone who has not given the same sacrifice come in and devalue them.

We have to determine for ourselves that we will, at all cost, protect the integrity of our leadership and ministry. We can then make the platform a place of sacrifice and honor. We are bringing a higher standard and dignity to the most visible part of our ministry.

Questions for Reflection

1. Do you have a practice of doing what you say, when you say, how you say?
2. Do people respect you and take you at your word?
3. Are you preserving the integrity of your platform ministry each week by your wise choices?
4. Do you sometimes think too highly of yourself and your abilities?

Next Steps for Success

1. Pray that God will make you a person of the highest integrity.
2. Make "Do what you say, when you say how you say" a personal motto for your life and teach this principle to someone.
3. Increase your leadership by thinking of yourself and your ambitions less and seek to help others be successful.

The Importance of the Basics

But seek first his kingdom and his righteousness,
and all these things will be given to you as well.

—Matthew 6:33(NIV)

EVERYTHING IN LIFE has a basic or fundamental function. In basketball, there are fundamental techniques to each game, such as dribbling, shooting, and passing. In playing the piano, there are fundamental practices, such as proper fingering, chord structures, and counting time. No matter how complex or how simple the basketball maneuver is or how complex or simple the piano piece is, the fundamentals remain. Complexities can be created and creativity can be explored, but nothing can ever take the place of the basics.

No matter where we are on our ministry journey, whether it is large and complex or small and simple, there are basic ministry principles that must never be forgotten. Keeping these few ministry basics as a part of our everyday perspective will be the basis and foundation for all other ministry practices.

Do Ministry for the Lord and for the People

Equipping people to do their best will require our best thinking and our best extra effort. It is one thing to do our best, get ourselves ready, and execute a task by ourselves. However, a completely different level of leadership and excellence is required to get others to do their best, to get them ready, and to help them execute the task.

In my mind, my wife and three young children illustrate this principle very well on Sunday mornings. Because of my Sunday morning schedule, I leave the house very early, and my wife has to manage the children alone. Before we had children, I would kiss my wife good-bye and head to church to prepare for the day. She would get up, get ready, and—since she sings with the praise team—head out the door to be in time for sound check. We had a good routine. However, now that we have children, my wife not only has to get herself ready, but she has to get three young children up, fed, dressed, and out the door, still in time for sound check. The simple task of getting ready for church has become much more difficult now that she has to prepare others as well as herself. So how does she do this week after week? She makes careful plans including the children and making sure that their needs are met while still meeting the demands of our shared ministry.

This same principle works in our ministry. We must think about what is best for those we lead. Our success as a leader is decided in large measure by our ability to see, grasp, and accomplish this principle. To the level that we love the people we are called to serve, we will prepare for ministry to them and with them. Our service and love for our people is a reflection of our love and relationship with the Lord. The more we know and love Him, the more we will seek to serve and prepare to lead and love others.

The Basics Must Be Attended to Constantly

The "extras" will not matter if they do not rest on the foundation of the "basics." We need to review constantly the basics of our ministry. Here is a list of the basics for our music ministry:

- Prayer
- Good communication
- Superior preparation
- Excellence in Sunday worship, morning and evening
- Excellence in rehearsals and rehearsal preparation
- Attention to detail
- Loving and leading people well
- Integrity

Whatever our basics may be, we must review them and make sure they are attended to in some way systematically. We can schedule time each week to give attention to these basic tenants. At my church, our staff is reminded of our basic commitments every week at staff meeting. The agenda has our basics printed at the top for us to see and evaluate. This systematic approach reminds us how important these matters are. Often, as a staff, we will review these basics and discuss how we are accomplishing them within our individual ministries.

In addition to establishing basics for our music ministry, we would do well to have a set of basics for our individual lives. Having a list of the basic priorities of our lives gives us focus. Even for volunteer music leaders or staff persons at a small church, the ability to lead ourselves well and focus on basics is even more critical.

Here is the list of my personal basics:

- Prayer, worship, and devotional time
- Family time

- Leadership development
- Worship planning
- Reading and writing
- School
- Exercise

These fundamentals are a priority in my schedule each week. Everything else flows from or supports these basics.

Always Be Prepared

Lack of preparation can never be hidden. Our cover will be blown at some point if we are trying just to get by unprepared. The idea "fake it till you make it" is not a good mentality for effective ministry. Stepping up to lead unprepared is not paying the price. Our desired end result will always be diminished. We cannot dream of a successful growing ministry but lack the ability to prepare and execute a plan adequately.

First, lack of preparation is a spiritual issue and shows a lack of discipline. If we come to a meeting, a rehearsal, or a worship service unprepared, we are demonstrating that we did not allocate the proper time or that we made bad choices with our time and efforts. Therefore, we did not take the necessary steps to be prepared. This behavior is ungodly and does not reflect good leadership.

Second, being unprepared shows a lack of love for our people. Unpreparedness frustrates and diminishes the value of our people and of our own ministry organization. We shortchange our ministry, weaken relationships, and diminish our leadership if we continually come to ministry unprepared.

A few small changes in our thinking and schedule can overcome unpreparedness and give us the time we need. Sometimes the answer lies with a lack of maturity or even selfishness. Other times we may need to deal with a lack of love and understanding of the purpose and role of a ministry leader.

Be Responsible and Accountable to the Whole

The success of our worship ministries will be largely determined by how we view our responsibility to the entire church body. We must see and understand what the Lord is doing within the church before we can understand how the Lord is leading and moving within our own area of ministry.

At my church, not only am I responsible for the nurturing and equipping of the people in the music ministry, but I am also involved in the welfare of the entire church family. I often have responsibilities that have more church-wide impact and focus beyond the music ministry.

The Walt Disney Company is a great example of how being responsible to the whole is critical to the success and health of the entire organization. It does not matter what position a person holds at a Walt Disney venue, everyone is a janitor. Why? Because everyone who works for the Disney company is concerned with the overall guest experience. So, for example, if someone works as a photographer on Main Street, USA, and is walking to his or her post for a shift and happens to see some trash on the ground, the trash must be picked up. Keeping trash off the walkways is everyone's job.

Leadership is being responsible to the whole, not just to ourselves. Self-preservation is the enemy of leadership and stands in the way of growth and excellence. We may not want to jump in and get involved out of fear of what others may think or because of the cost involved. To see what needs to be done and not act forfeits our leadership completely. To see and not act is not to see at all.

In the book *The Oz Principle*, the authors offer a new definition of *accountability* that embodies the kind of ownership of the whole that we have been discussing. Consider this new definition:

> Accountability.
> A personal choice to rise above one's circumstances and demonstrate the ownership necessary for achieving desired results—to See It, Own It, Solve It, and Do It.

Such a perspective embraces both current and future efforts rather than reactive and historical explanations. Armed with this new definition of *accountability*, we can help ourselves and others do everything possible to both overcome difficult circumstances and achieve desired results.[1]

When we are responsible to the whole organization, we will naturally obtain the perspective of those we serve every week—our choir members and our congregation. We will be personally invested in making sure that they have an environment and an experience that maximizes their opportunity to engage in worship.

We must constantly remember the basics and always act from them. If we ever get away from the foundational functions of ministry, no measure of growth will be long lasting or have the greatest kingdom-growth impact.

Questions for Reflection

1. How long has it been since you have reviewed the fundamentals of your ministry?
2. Are you doing the fundamentals well? If not, why [not]? If yes, how can you improve your skills?

---

1   Craig Hickman, Tom Smith, and Roger Connors, *The Oz Principle: Getting Results through Individual and Organizational Accountability*, Rev ed. (New York, NY: Portfolio Trade, 2010), 47.

3. Are you consistently prepared to lead your people every day? What are some things that you can do to be better prepared?

4. In what ways do you portray your accountability to your entire organization?

Next Steps for Success

1. Make a list of the fundamentals of your ministry. Place them in priority order and then begin to work on them one at a time.

2. If you are not good at organizing yourself so that you are always well prepared, ask for help. Contact someone whom you know is organized and seems always to be prepared for meetings, activities, and commitments.

3. Walk around your church or ministry area. Take note of some things that need attention. Now do something about it!

SECTION II

Essential Practices for Success

7

Raising the Standards

> Whatever you do, work at it with all your
> heart, as working for the Lord,
> not for men, since you know that you
> will receive an inheritance
> from the Lord as a reward. It is the
> Lord Christ you are serving.
>
> —Colossians 3:23–24 (NIV)

WE NEED TO start with a logical question: What are standards? We could suggest that standards are simply a measurement of values. I recently asked one of my staff members to give me his definition of the term *standards*. He thought for a while, and then he offered me this insightful definition: "An attainable expectation of functional and practical quality determined by values."[1] Wow! Basically, this means that our lives and ministries will reflect the things that we think are most important. If high musical quality is our standard, we will spend the majority of our time working on musical notes and rhythms to create the outcome we hold most important. If we value warmth and fellowship, we will most

---

1   Justin Chades, Interview, 2013.

likely create an environment of fun, fellowship, and conversation. If we value leadership, we will train and grow leaders.

The questions are these: What are my personal standards? What are my organizational standards? And how do I continually raise the standards in my life and ministry? We need to be able to answer these questions in order to have a successful and vibrant ministry.

Many of us are afraid to raise the standards within our organizations. We can be gripped with fear that no one will accept a new standard, and people will quit. It is true that not everyone will move to the level of the standards we set, but my experience is that most will gladly rise to the new level of requirements. People ultimately want to be involved in something of value. They want to know that they are not wasting their time, and they want a sense of challenge and investment. To continually challenge our people means to continually raise the standards.

One of the things that I value is people being committed to the work of ministry and called to serve our congregation through our music ministry. I knew that if I developed an environment of people who love the Lord and are passionately fulfilling their calling, then we would, in return, have a dynamic and passion-filled ministry. One of the ways that I started is with membership requirements for the choir and orchestra. I wanted to make sure that the people who are involved in the music ministry are really called and committed to service. So, over the years, I have continually advanced the requirements for membership in the choir and orchestra. When I inherited this music ministry, it was really easy to become a member. Anyone who attended one rehearsal was eligible to sing or play on Sunday morning. My first change was to add another rehearsal requirement. Now people had to attend two rehearsals in a row before they were eligible to sing on a Sunday morning. This change was not a difficult advancement, was received well, and was understandable because of the difficulty of the music that we were rehearsing.

Eventually, I knew there was another layer of membership that we needed to add. We needed a way to explain our ministry, why we do the things we do and what the new expectations are. We wanted people to be called to be in the ministry before they started singing or playing on Sundays. With great hesitation, I added a music orientation session. I hesitated because I did not want to make it too complex for people to enter the music ministry. I was afraid that if I made the process too difficult, people would find it not worth the effort, and the pace of our growth would slow down. But I knew that we needed to rise to a new level of ministry, so I decided to try it. I was thrilled to find that the music orientation session did not slow growth; it sped it up. People appreciated the information and explanation of the expectations before they made the decision to join the choir or orchestra. In fact, I found out that one of our attrition factors was because people did not realize the complexity and requirements of our ministry before they joined.

With this step in place, we narrowed the attrition rate drastically. We saw a significant increase in average attendance and overall stability and consistency of our weekly ministry. After the addition of music orientation (held once a month), the next risk I took in raising the standards was to have seasons of open and closed enrollment. I needed to put something like this in place to protect the integrity of our large-scale Christmas show and our Easter programming. We work for months on both of these special seasons, and we had nothing to protect us from someone deciding to join at the last minute. So after careful thought, I decided to close enrollment the first of October of every year. This policy prevents anyone from joining the choir or orchestra until after our Christmas show is over. I open enrollment again the first of the year and then close it again several weeks before Easter to protect that special program. Enrollment is opened again after Easter is over. I was warned by some of my colleagues that this policy could potentially detract people from wanting to join the music ministry, and I could miss out on enrollment opportunities. But I knew I needed to do something, so I decided to give it a try. Again, to my surprise, every time we open enrollment, we see a big rush of people wanting to join. Every time I have raised the standard and enacted a new policy, the change has added value and strength to our organization and has protected our people and the hard work that they do each week. This progression has served to be a win-win for our ministry and the people who make it up. Today our system remains the same, except that I just recently added a third week to the required rehearsal attendance for people seeking membership.

Here is my encouragement:

1. Continually seek to raise the standards.
2. Seek win-win options for the organization and the people who make it up.
3. Always explain the why of planned policy changes.
4. Be consistent with changes and make them an expectation.
5. Policies should be in place to add value to ministry and remove the frustration for people already participating.
6. Do not be afraid to raise the standards. It can seem scary, but we should always seek to do ministry with excellence.

As a result of raising standards, here is what will happen:
1. *Almost everyone will step up and meet the new standard.* People want to be challenged. They like to be a part of something that is bigger than themselves and adds value to their lives. People will give us a significant amount of

their time and resources if they feel that it is a beneficial use of their time and is making an impact.

2. *Some people will not rise to meet the standard and leave our ministry.* We cannot stop this from happening, but we also cannot let this fact stop us from moving our ministry forward. The truth is that we really do not want people in our ministry who cannot meet the standards. They will cause trouble and be a negative force as long as they do not see the benefit of the new standard.

3. *We will attract a different mind-set of people.* Good musicians attract good musicians. High-expectation ministries attract high-output people. The standards will naturally act as a weeding-out process, saving heartache in the future. We are being proactive in creating the successful environment that we want.

4. *All strong leadership that seeks to raise any standard will have to pay a price.* There is a price to pay for successful ministry. It does not come easy, or else everyone would have it. We must be willing to do what is necessary to elevate our level of ministry and influence. This price may be paid in losing some people, or it may be paid within the details necessary to make a new standard necessary. It may mean more administrative work and accountability for us each week.

5. *We will gain respect and followership from our people.* Our choir, orchestra, and band members will appreciate the value that we place on them and the ministry. They will know that we care for and love them. They will respond to our leadership by giving us their trust. They will gladly follow us and do what is necessary to move the ministry forward.

Questions for Reflection

1. What are some areas of my ministry where I need to raise the standards?
2. What will happen in our organization if I require more from our people?
3. What price am I willing to pay for a ministry of success?

Next Steps for Success

1. Gather a few key leaders and discuss some areas in your ministry that need improving or changing. Develop a systematic plan for implementation.
2. Prepare your people by telling them that it is time to take the ministry to the next level.
3. Set deadlines for your goals and begin working on bringing everyone along.

Attention to Detail

Each one should use whatever gift he has received to serve others, faithfully administering God's grace in its varied forms.

—1 Peter 4:10 (NIV)

ATTENTION TO DETAIL is an important discipline that helps make a good ministry a great ministry. I am already assuming that we are seeking to love well the people in our ministry and church and that we are striving to have an impactful ministry. An eye for detail stems from the love that we have for our ministry participants. We could say to ourselves, "I love my people, but I'm not a detail person." If that is true, maybe this admonition will help: if we want to move our ministries forward, we must discipline ourselves to become a detail person. Dealing with details does come more naturally to some than others. But I am convinced that anyone can develop the eye for details if he or she chooses to do so and puts in place a system to help with this organizational necessity. The greater the detail of an organization, the more special, significant, and impactful that organization can become. It is also true that the more detailed a life, the richer (more meaningful) that life becomes.

A detailed ministry/life does not necessarily mean a more complex ministry/life. It simply means that the steps and processes are well-thought-out and have meaning and purpose. Even someone with the simplest ministry can pay attention to significant details. When we begin to look at our ministries through the eyes of those who have to endure it every week or get to experience it every week, we will begin to care more about the details.

Interestingly enough, every layer of detail adds a layer of significance, no matter how it is applied. Take worship planning for instance. The beauty of a service can lie within the details. Most ministers provide an order of worship for each service; that is fairly common. But let me suggest an added layer of detail by creating a technical script or flowchart for services. What elements are we planning? How are we communicating important information to our congregations? How well do the songs flow together? Do the congregational worship elements support the topic or theme of the message? Have we thought through song transitions, keys (can the congregation sing it)? What about the times of all the elements? The music selections, sound, media, dress, lighting, transitions, order, flow, and preparation are all details that can play a significant role in a worship experience and must be considered if we want to move to a different level of ministry impact and inspiration with our congregations.

Some may raise the question, Can't we worship without all the fluff? The answer: of course, we can. A believer can worship anytime, anyplace, in any environment.

About six years ago, I led an evangelistic music mission trip to New York City. We partnered with a few small churches in that city to help where needed, and we were asked to join one of the church's worship team and lead worship on Sunday morning. We got to the school auditorium where the church service was held ahead of time to be as prepared as possible. However, our idea of prepared and the church's idea of prepared were two different things. Everything was late, everybody was late, and everything leading up to the service's start time seemed thrown together. I was a bit frazzled, and my team seemed somewhat bewildered. We felt that we were unprepared to do our very best ministry. However, when the service finally started, we worshiped the Lord, and it was a great service. Although we had a good day of worship and praise, this church did not have a sustainable organization for growth. I later found out that the worship team had a lot of turnover because of frustration and burnout. Our team was relieved because of how the service turned out, but they were less than impressed with the frustration that they had to endure in order to do something that they love and are trained to do. So, indeed, the Lord can be worshiped in any circumstance; but in order to make the most of the efforts of the participants and to be the best stewards of what we have, attention to details is necessary to grow and build a strong and healthy environment where people feel consistently equipped and prepared to give their best. I wonder how many of our choir, instrumental, or praise team members feel the same way in our ministries as our mission team felt when we were in New York.

Each element that we add to our services for the purpose of edifying the body of Christ to worship the Lord in Spirit and in truth can and should be pleasing to the Lord. So to whatever our resources are—whether we are in a church with no instruments, a church with just a piano, a church with maybe an organ or a keyboard, or a church with a full orchestra or band—those resources should be used to their fullest and should be managed in such a way that they bring glory to God and aid the people of God in their worship. "The greatest and the best is the responsibility of every man and woman of God."[1] We help our music participants

---

1   Engstrom, *Pursuit of Excellence*, 18.

give their best by paying attention to detail and equipping them well to do their best. As a worship minister, it is our responsibility to equip the people of God to do the ministry of the church. We are empowerers. We are encouragers. We are growers.

If you are a person who is not very detailed, here are a few suggestions:

Start at the End

In his book *The 7 Habits of Highly Effective People*, Steven Covey says it this way, "Begin with the end in mind."[2] What do we want the end result of whatever we are working on to look like? Suppose we are planning our annual Christmas program. Our usual routine could look like this: First, listen to all the latest Christmas musicals or cantatas coming out this year. Choose the one with the most songs that are singable for our choir or with tunes that we like. Next, we pick our soloists. Then we start rehearsals about mid-October. In mid-November, we might put a notice in the bulletin asking everyone to bring a friend. We move the pulpit for emphasis, add a few ferns that we borrowed from someone in the choir, and then we perform the musical. In the end, what have we accomplished? We completed a seasonal ministry task. Everyone in the choir was proud of singing those different arrangements of the songs, and there was a good turnout from everybody in the church. Another year finished.

Now, if we begin with the end in mind, think kingdom impact. Here are some things that our team will think about when planning for the Christmas program:

1. Why are we doing this event?

---

2   Stephen R. Covey, *The 7 Habits of Highly Effective People: Powerful Lessons in Personal Change*, Anniversary ed. (New York, NY: Simon & Schuster, 2013), 95.

2. Who do we want to come?

3. How can we get as many people as possible to come?

4. How can we generate prospects for our church?

5. How do we want our target audience to respond during and at the conclusion of our presentation?

6. What resources and elements can we use to help our audience respond in the way that we would like for them to?

7. How much time do we need to produce the musical?

8. Who do we need to involve to produce the musical?

9. How will we follow up with those who come to invite them to come back?

10. What will we invite them back to?

Answering these ten questions can make a definitive difference in the outcome of our musicals. At our church, the end result is reaching people for Christ and changing lives. That is why we ask those kinds of questions. We decided a long time ago that we did not want to waste valuable time and resources to put on a musical just for the enjoyment of our church family. Instead, we want to focus on bringing the hope of Christ to as many people as possible. When these ten questions are thoroughly and honestly answered, they act as a guide to all the details. I guarantee that answering these questions with the end results in mind can put any music ministry on the right track to have a successful and meaningful event with kingdom impact.

Make Lists

People often laugh at me because I am constantly making lists. I have a terrible memory and have to discipline myself to remember details. Because I value the details and am committed to them, I have a systematic approach to carrying them out. A little pocket notebook, a smartphone, any number of tools will work. It does not matter where lists are, just that they are made. I make lists every day of things I see that need attention—things that I think could make an experience better for my choir, orchestra, or the congregation. I write it all down. The small details, the simple thoughts, the big ideas—I write them down. Later I take my lists, sort through them, and prioritize.

Seek the Right Perspective

I am trying to teach my team how to think outside of themselves. We are servants, but so often we get the idea reversed. We can get blinded to the fact that we are here to equip others to do the work of the ministry instead of us. Because of our poor thinking, we can walk through our tasks and be doing them with excellence; and through it all, we forget about how our decisions affect the people we are serving.

Here is a simple example: Our media team was recently installing some new lighting on our stage to add some color to the walls and banisters. When I walked into the room, the lit stage looked gorgeous. It had splashes of color and was very tastefully done. When I started to leave the room, I happened to walk out the door that our choir members walk out of every Sunday. As I was walking, one of the lights already in place blinded me as I reached the stage exit door. I knew then that the placement of the light would not work because all our choir and orchestra members would have to have retina replacement surgery every week after coming off the stage. I mentioned this problem to our team up in the booth. Their response was normal and something that we have all heard before: "They'll just have to live with it."

The next Sunday arrived, and the well-thought-out lighting scheme looked incredible. The choir and orchestra led impeccably well, and then it was time to exit the stage. We had a human train wreck at the doors. The light blinded the choir members so badly that they could not see the door. They put their hands up over their eyes and ran into one another trying to get out! It was an embarrassing moment and took away from the worship experience we just had. Instead of staying in the moment, that poorly placed light caused a wave of grumble and dissatisfaction. We did not serve our choir and orchestra members well because we did not think on their behalf; the poorly placed light did more damage than good.

During our evaluations of that service and the choir and orchestra responses, we were able to keep the light in the same place and program that particular light to go out when the choir and orchestra made their exit. Both the lighting crew and choir and orchestra members were happy. It was a win-win scenario. This problem is just a silly illustration but a true one. We make decisions every day that affect others, and we do not even think about, nor do we care, how others will respond. This is selfish and not the leadership required for successful ministry.

Again, let me say that I am convinced: attention to detail is one of the most important differences between good ministry and a great ministry. In their book, *The Disney Way*, Bill Capodagli and Lynn Jackson devote an entire chapter to explaining how the Walt Disney Company, as well as other companies, stands out above the rest because of their consistent and systematic approach to details. Many leaders can fall victim to painting the big picture for their organization but leave the details undone. Soon the big vision fades away because no attention was given to the details necessary to bring the big picture to reality. "Paying attention to the little things is what turns the vision into a top-quality product or an outstanding service."[3] Walt Disney himself realized that attention to detail was the key to the complete realization of his dreams.

We all have dreams that we want to accomplish. Hopefully, we are aware of the vision that God has given us for our ministries and are seeking obediently to accomplish our purpose. May I say that we will never reach our full potential if we do not exercise the discipline of paying attention to details?

Paying attention to the details not only means that we will be seeking to execute our ministry with excellence and in a way that fully equips our people for ministry, but it also means that we will be measuring results. Doing an evaluation brings us full circle to my first point of starting at the end. At the conclusion of our Christmas or Easter event, or our choir retreat, or even simply a choir rehearsal, we must evaluate and measure the results: Did we accomplish our goals? If so, how well? If no, why not? Did people respond how we wanted them to? These types of questions provide information to help us evaluate our successes, understand our weaknesses, and bring significance and meaning to everything that we do.

Do not misunderstand. Attention to detail and following through with those details are not magic solutions to having a thriving ministry, but they are a very important piece of the puzzle. However, I have found that those who love enough and are thoughtful enough to pay attention to the details usually possess many of the other qualities and characteristics that are helpful when leading a growing ministry.

---

3   Bill Capodagli and Lynn Jackson, *The Disney Way: Harnessing the Management Secrets of Disney in Your Company*, Revised ed. (New York: McGraw-Hill Education, 2007), 201.

Questions for Reflection

1. Do I naturally have an eye for detail? If so, am I using that ability to better serve my congregation and ministry participants? If not, how will I develop eyes for detail?
2. How is my lack of detail frustrating the people I am trying to lead?

Next Steps for Success

1. Spend time detailing your worship services. Develop a detailed order of worship that specifies times, personnel, actions, queues, instruments, mics used, measure numbers, etc. Be as detailed as possible.
2. Ask your leaders what kind of details they would like to see receive attention.
3. Develop a habit of writing down everything that you see that needs improving. This will help you develop an eye for detail.

9

Scheduling for Success

If we progress in the economy of time, we are learning to live.
If we fail here, we fail everywhere.

—J. Oswald Sanders[1]

WHAT GETS SCHEDULED gets done. I have met very few people, if any, who have the ability to maneuver through a productive day with nothing scheduled. Those who would rather not live by the calendar have a greater chance of wasting time during the day and making less of a contribution to life, family, and ministry. In his book *Spiritual Leadership*, J. Oswald Sanders says, "We are not responsible for our endowments or natural abilities, but we are responsible for the strategic use of time."[2] What he means is that there are things beyond our control, but we are the only ones who can make the best use of our time.

Scheduling can be simple and quick. It may take some time to get things organized at the beginning, but soon we will realize that a little bit of time completing a schedule will make for productive days and weeks. We may start with scheduling things that are

1   Sanders, *Spiritual Leadership, 94.*
2   Ibid.

the most detailed—things that must be done. Then the layer of scheduling can be our monthly calendar. Pretty soon, we have the important information that we need to do some long-range planning for next year. *Yes!* I said *next year*. In our ministry, we do something called one-thousand-day planning. This view allows us to see the big picture of the next few years in broad strokes and then how each decision and calendared event trickles down to the month, weeks, and then days. I can see on the calendar when major church events are taking place and then begin to strategize around them. I can even plan my family vacations far in advance.

It does not matter what the size or scope of our ministry is; we can be good planners. We all know there are some things that we will have on our calendar throughout the year. If we had a blank calendar right now, we could write down Easter and Christmas for sure. If there are other specific events that we know will be on our church calendar, we can go ahead and write them in. Now, begin to think backward. For instance, think about Christmas. If the Christmas program will be in early December, we can back up three to five months to begin our Christmas music. We may plan to begin rehearsing our Christmas music with the band or orchestra in September. When will we need to order the music? Once we figure that out, we write "Order Christmas music" on our calendar. Before we know what to order, we have to listen to several choices so we will need to know when to start listening to music.

If we just continue to think in reverse from each event and note each step necessary to accomplish the event and begin to schedule the details, our calendar will start to take shape, and then our days will start to have meaning, order, and pupose.

Scheduling is very effective when done thoroughly, with as much detail as possible—but it is not complete until it is shared. I take a systematic approach to communicating my schedule. First, my ministry assistant and my wife know everything on my calendar. I review my calendar with them weekly. Second, I let my staff know strategic things on my calendar. Third, I let my lay leadership know strategic items and events on my calendar. Fourth, I let my pastor know strategic things on my calendar. He rarely asks, but I just offer the information in an e-mail periodically to him.

Now, why would I share my calendar or strategic scheduling with so many people? Simply put—*trust*. This simple act of keeping a schedule and sharing it offers an insight to my circle of people. It lets them know that I have direction and have given thought to my days, weeks, months, and years. It allows people an easier window to see into my life and respect my time. But most of all, it provides a basis for followership. Believe it or not, people want to follow leaders whom they trust, leaders on mission, leaders who are good stewards of their time. Over the years, my scheduling has acted as a strong statement about my leadership and my commitment to time management and ministry impact.

On my first days on staff at Westside, I was warned by a few staff members and some others within the organization to be sure to learn to say no because the church would rob me of my family time. I cautiously listened and certainly realized that we were in a high-expectation, high-output ministry organization. But what I learned was that the only way the organization could steal my time was if I allowed it to. So I quickly became as organized as possible to prevent events or felt expectations from running my life and ruining my family. "Our problem is not too little time but making better use of the time we have."[3] There are always ministry seasons that demand more of my time than others, such as Christmas and Easter, but I rarely find myself feeling overextended and spending countless hours in the office. My kids know who I am, and my wife does not feel neglected or second-rate to my work, and we

---

3   Ibid.

have a vibrant and growing worship ministry. I contribute much of that to scheduling.

Any ministry of any size can become overwhelming and demanding of our energy and efforts. No matter the size of our ministry, scheduling is key to high kingdom impact and ministry success. If we fail to keep a schedule and calendar, here is what will happen or is already happening to us:

1. *People will not respect our time.* We will always have those who pop their heads in to speak to us or have an urgent word, and we will notice that people are constantly snagging us to do this or that. People's assumption is that we are flexible enough in our schedule that we can spend time with them anytime they ask. They will unintentionally pull us away from necessary tasks that are important for us to accomplish.

2. *Our circumstances control our day.* Because we do not have a schedule guiding our day, we will easily allow immediate circumstances to derail us from the most important things. We will constantly be battling for more time. We will end the day and will have been everywhere and done everything other than what we had intended to do. This practice ultimately leads to late nights at the office trying to get things done, needlessly robbing us of precious time with our family. This habit will result in tension at home and burnout in our ministry.

3. *We are rarely satisfied with our daily output and often feel unaccomplished.* Just like a budget for our money, if we do not keep a budget of our time, we will not realize what we are spending it on and we will waste it. At the end of the day, it is always gratifying to see where we have invested our time and that we have made the best of our day. When we are not keeping a good schedule or budget of our time,

we will often end our day empty, frustrated, and feeling unaccomplished. Again we may feel the need to spend additional hours in the office to try to make ourselves feel as if we have put in a good day's work.

4. *We are not leading our people well.* This neglect is probably one of the biggest tragedies of not keeping a calendar and schedule for our time. If we are not leading ourselves well, then we will have missed opportunities of love and leadership for our people.

5. *Our family or relationships will suffer.* Ultimately, our relationships will suffer because of our poor planning and management of our time. There have been many spouses and children who have fallen victim to the minister who has not understood the importance of mastering the discipline and practice of keeping a schedule for their lives and ministry. We understand that sacrifices will have to be made by a ministry family. But we should not neglect to plan and execute our schedule well and then blame it on ministry demands. This confusion not only places unnecessary tension within our relationships, but it also breeds resentment and jealousy toward the church and ministry work in general.

Keeping a schedule and carefully thinking through our days, weeks, months, and years primarily reflects? the love we have for the people we serve, including our family. Knowing what we are working toward each day brings about gratification and clarity of focus. Keeping a schedule will maximize our potential for success and make a difference for the cause of Christ.

Beware of playing busy. One time, I shared the important principles within this chapter with a staff member as they came on our staff. They completely misunderstood the concept and instead of filling their schedule with meaningful and productive objectives to get things done, they used the calendar to cover their laziness and schedule their "playtime." Do you think this worked? Nope! It did not work even a little bit. It did not take long for people to realize that this person was playing busy. He had no results to show for his full calendar. We are only fooling ourselves and allowing opportunities for life impact to slip by with a fake schedule.

Questions for Reflection

1. Do I feel in control of my daily schedule? If no, why not?
2. Do I believe that I am making the most of every opportunity that God gives me?
3. What can I do today to make sure that I am being a good steward of my time?

Next Steps for Success

1. Ask the Lord to give you wisdom concerning how you should organize your days, weeks, months, and years.
2. Develop a scheduling system that holds you accountable for your time.
3. Start communicating your schedule to those who need to know how you are using your time.

10

Developing Successful Systems

A bad system will beat a good person every time.

—W. Edwards Deming[1]

EVEN THE MOST creative and intelligent leaders among us will have a difficult time moving to a higher level of ministry influence if we fail to approach our ministries systematically. What do I mean by *systematically*? I mean a well-thought-out and thoroughly planned approach to the order of events, rehearsals, processes, days, weeks, months, and years.

"Systems create beliefs that create behaviors."[2] What are the beliefs that we want for our ministry or organization? What are the beliefs that we want our congregation to have about worship? What are the beliefs that we want our choir to have? Whatever they are, we must build a system to support our desired results. A systematic approach to our everyday ministry activity is critical in the process of moving from survival to success and significance. I have heard people say, "I'm not a systems person." I certainly do not want to offend or mean to be rude, but that statement is

---

1 W. Edward Deming, source unknown.
2 Tony Bridwell, Interview, 2013.

sometimes said out of ignorance, potentially reflects arrogance, and could be an indicator that there may be a fundamental misunderstanding of God's systematic design and process for growth and life. All of God's creation and nature run on a system. If we do not learn to approach ministry in a systematic way, nothing has a chance of moving forward.

There is never a week that goes by when my ministry system does not aid me in decision-making. Just recently, I was talking with a fellow worship pastor who asked me how I deal with people who are not interested in getting plugged into the worship ministry and just want to sing a solo or who have the wrong motives when singing. He wondered if I encounter this issue often. I told him, "Well, it is never easy to tell people who want to sing solos that they cannot sing. So I don't." He had this funny look on his face in response to my answer. But then I added, "I just explain to them the system to which they will have to commit if they want to sing." After potential soloists realize the price they will have to pay to be eligible to sing, they make the decision for themselves. There is typically a few times a year where this situation comes up.

In our ministry, one of our values is to have a strongly committed group of people who love and worship the Lord. I decided a long time ago to set up a system that would help me produce that kind of environment and would guide people's behaviors to accomplish the atmosphere that I desired. First, I began by raising the standards of commitment necessary for participation in our music ministry. I do not want anyone to have the opportunity to put me in a difficult position by asking to sing a solo when the person is not even a part of our church or ongoing ministry. I do not think it is fair to let someone stand on our platform and lead our people in worship when he or she has not paid the price to do so.

My first systematic policy was to make it a requirement that persons must be active members of our choir or orchestra before they can be eligible to audition to sing a solo. I explained this step to my choir and orchestra one night at the conclusion of rehearsal. I told them that I valued the hard work and the sacrifice that they make each week to our shared ministry. I mentioned that I did not think it was good leadership to allow someone to use our credibility to sing a solo if that person had not spent the time in rehearsal and in service with our people. I introduced our new policy of making the choir and orchestra ministry the central hub in which everything else would flow. I emphasized that this policy meant that people would have to be a member of the choir or orchestra before they were eligible to audition to sing a solo or participate in any other capacity. The choir and orchestra members overwhelmingly agreed because, at that moment, I gave value to them and their efforts in the music ministry. They had a sense of pride that I would not allow someone to rob them of their credibility.

Over the years, our policy has evolved and grown. As I explained in chapter 5, this system helps bring integrity to our platform ministry. In order to be a member of our choir and orchestra, people must attend three successive rehearsals, as well as graduate from a required music orientation class. Once they have completed these expectations, then they are eligible to sing in the choir or play in the orchestra during our services. Once members, they then have the opportunity to audition for the solo roster. If they pass the audition, then they are up to a three-month probation period before they are scheduled to sing the first solo. After the probation period, they will be scheduled to sing on Wednesday night for our midweek Bible study.

So the systematic layers protect me from the spontaneous questions that I get from people who are not a vested member in our organization. I never have to tell them they cannot sing.

I simply tell them the process that they have to go through in order to sing. I share with them our system. If their hearts are in the right place, they will gladly embrace and begin the process. If they are not interested, they will not pursue our ministry. This system may seem to be a complicated process that would scare a lot of people away. I once thought that too. I was scared to death to make a music orientation class a requirement for membership. I thought that it would deter people from entering the ministry. Not so at all! Do you know what I discovered? Implementing this step added value, and only those who were really sensing a call to be in the music ministry engaged in the process. Actually, this system slowed down the attrition rate tremendously. Not only were we adding people systematically, we were keeping more of them. In time, we have grown a consistent membership that is solid and unified. I was able to accomplish my goal of having a strong, committed group of people who love one another and want to worship the Lord.

There are many other systems that we can put in place for things such as attendance, rehearsals, sound checks, and various other functions of ministry. Let me make some suggestions for developing a system that will move our ministries forward.

Establish a List of Priorities for Ministry

Our systems need to be built around our priorities and values. I value a powerful ministry full of people who love and want to worship the Lord. I knew that if I wanted to attract the kind of people who are serious about worship, I needed to create a system that supported that priority.

Define the System

A system is a process of events with a purpose. Every step within the process should be in place for a reason. To define the system, begin with the end in mind. Make a list of the desired results and then work backward from there. Write down the necessary steps that it will take to gain the desired results or behaviors. Then work through it, make necessary adjustments, and implement. Be sure that every step has a good rationale and supports the desired priority.

Communicate the System

Communicating is the scary part because once we start to talk about our system, there is no going back. Most people never make it to this point because they chicken out. It is at this communication step when we begin to hear and see how people will respond to the new standard or process. There is a trick that can help with this step. Do not walk through the system-making process alone. Early on, we should tell a few trusted people what we want to accomplish and let them brainstorm with us. Let them help develop the steps in our organization's systematic approach. We should avoid keeping things all to ourselves before sharing with the greater whole. We need to get people to walk with us along the way. Then when it comes time to tell the choir what the new expectations will be, we can more likely ensure that we will already have some people who agree with us. If we have a lay ministry team in place, we can walk them through the expectations and allow them to respond. Understand that their responses will be similar to the responses at large. We must be careful to listen and take notes and be willing to make adjustments.

Be Consistent When Carrying Out the System

A system will work for us only if we work the system. If there are thoughtful processes in place to accomplish a certain work, then it is important that the system is used to build strength and consistency within the organization.

Not too long ago, a woman moved to our town and joined our church. She had been a faithful member of the choir and praise team at my previous church in Alabama. I knew that she had a great heart for ministry and would be a great asset to our praise team, so I was excited when she and her husband joined Westside. I probably could have plugged her in immediately with no worries as to her contribution to our ministry. But instead, I was up-front with her and explained our organizational system and told her that she would have to go through the process for the sake of the integrity of our ministry. She completely understood and was thrilled to get plugged in to the ministry and get to know everyone.

Because I placed the whole organization before the desires of my own heart, I protected our choir and protected her and myself from the possible fallout that could have come from everyone else who had to go through the system.

When it was the right time to add her, everyone was delighted that she was joining our team, and there has never been a question about our previously having served together or that I was showing favoritism.

This experience is just a small example, but one that I feel is relative. We can all probably think of ways that our system has the potential to help us when used properly or harm us when neglected.

Final Thoughts on Systems

The purpose of systems and processes are to aid and protect people in ministry. They are meant to foster growth and unity within the body and can create strength and harmony. However, systems can also be choking and damaging to an organization if the systems in place are not meaningful and helpful in fulfilling the overall desired result. There are two reasons for this kind of damage: First, the systems can be put into place because of insecurities and wrong motives. Second, the systems can become antiquated and in need of revision. A system should never hurt or hinder ministry and relationships. Proper systems are freeing and aid in growth and should never seem pharisaic. Finally, systems should be refined often. As we outgrow our system or change our values, the system must grow and evolve as well.

Questions for Reflection

1. Do you currently have a ministry system in place? Is it effective?
2. Do you often find that you are wasting time and energy with no movement forward and constant frustration among your leaders and people?
3. Have you been resistant to approach ministry systematically because it intimidates you or because you have been victim of a bad system?
4. What kind of ministry do you want to develop? How do you want people to respond and act within your ministry?

Next Steps for Success

1. Begin to list your processes for worship ministry members. Discover what holes exist in your current system and take action steps to fill the gaps.
2. If your system has bad processes, revamp them. Systems are only as good as the processes that make them up.
3. Start from entry to exit and walk your way through the steps of an individual within your ministry. Seek to add value at every stage. This examination will help reinforce the behaviors that you want to see from your people.
4. Communicate your system processes. Be able to answer the why for each process.

11

Successful Ministry Organization and Administration

Victory lies in the organization of the nonobvious.

—Marcus Aurelius[1]

WHEN I CAME on staff at Westside, this statement made by our then senior pastor Dr. Gary Crawford intrigued me: "Organization puts us in the best possible position to be used by the Holy Spirit."[2] I had never heard such a statement, nor did I realize the full impact of it until I saw it work for myself. Now I use this quotation from Dr. Crawford all the time. If we want to be used fully to our maximum potential, then we will need to organize our lives in a way that allows this to happen. As a musician, I am a naturally creative person, and organization is not a natural inclination in my life. Therefore, I had to create a discipline for organization. If we desire to move ourselves or any organization forward, we will be able to do so only based on the capacity of our organization.

---

1   Marcus Aurelius, source unknown.
2   Dr. Gary Crawford, Interview, 2012.

For example, an organization for 25 people in the choir will not be as complex as an organization for 225 people. As our organization grows, so does our organizational structure. The size of a building is determined by the foundational structure that is in place to support it. No matter how large or small our ministry, we will need to grow our systematic organizational structure in order to support additional people. From a spiritual perspective, the more organized we are, the greater capacity for us to make kingdom impact. Notice, I did not say *size*. Ministry size does not determine the greater impact. I know worship pastors in large churches who are not making a significant impact in people's lives or for the kingdom of Christ. They struggle also with understanding the necessary steps in moving from survival every week to having a successful transformational ministry.

I was recently in a local family-owned carpet-and-tile business in our town. The showroom was very nice, and several employees were buzzing around. After waiting awhile for help, I realized that no one even noticed that I was there or that I needed help. Finally, I was taken to the back where I selected the carpet that I wanted. I was told it would be ready for pickup in a few days after it had been edged. When I returned to pick up my carpet, I saw that they had pulled the wrong carpet to be bound and edged. The manager apologized for the mix-up and explained that their business had grown so fast that they were not working as effectively and efficiently as they once had. They were frustrating one another in the office and were making mistakes with their customers.

This carpet-buying experience reminded me that systems constantly have to be tended and recalibrated to support the organization that they are trying to serve. An organization will never successfully move beyond the system that supports it. If we want to grow our ministries, then we must develop the system and infrastructure that allow them to expand.

As worship pastors, we should know everything there is to know about our ministry and everything that directly or indirectly affects our ministry. For example, not only do I keep track of the attendance of my ministry, but I also keep track of worship and Bible study attendance. Bible study highly affects our music ministry; in the same way, the choir affects Bible study. No one is an island; no ministry is independent. All church ministries are connected and woven together to enhance the strength of the whole. Because the growth of my ministry is important to me, I have learned to care about the growth of the other ministries in the church. This concern fosters a *team* approach of shared ministry. Once we understand that the success of the whole equals the success of our individual ministries, then we will think, plan, and organize differently. We will begin to make decisions that will be a win-win for all ministries. We will make decisions with context and lasting impact.

Here is where the rubber meets the road, and the principles become the practiced. The next few sections of this chapter will discuss some of my organizational practices and the reasons behind them—practices that have proven to work well for me. I realize that everyone must come up with his or her own organization for success. My organization has evolved over the years, and I know that it will continue to do so. Read these sections with the applicable principles in mind.

Daily Schedules/To-Do Lists

Our daily activity and productivity greatly increase when we are organized and operate from a task or to-do list. Someone who does not like to-do lists or refuses to use them, I believe, will be limited in growth as an individual, a leader, and a minister of the Gospel. Instead of having control over the day, the day will have control over us. We will find ourselves moving aimlessly from one thing to another, completing very few projects and always feeling unfulfilled. We will find ourselves saying, "I just don't have time to do what needs to be done." There are certain times, even with the best planning, when we can overextend ourselves, but this situation typically points back to poor scheduling. In general, this overextension should not be true of the leaders who have control of their schedule. In his book *Spiritual Leadership*, J. Oswald Sanders says this, "A leader will seldom say, 'I don't have the time.' Such an excuse is usually the refuge of a small-minded and inefficient person. Each of us has the time to do the whole will of God for our lives."[3]

The discipline of keeping a to-do list can revolutionize our day and week. We will be able to see where we spend our time, when we can make appointments, and how to schedule the important tasks that only we can do. Within the scope of our ministry, we will have several schedules helping us keep track of many things. The larger and more complex the ministry organization, the more schedules, calendars, and lists will have to be maintained.

First, I have the church calendar with everything involving church-wide events. This calendar helps me stay contextual in my planning and thinking.

Next, I have my personal and ministry annual calendar. This calendar has events that pertain to my particular life, family, and ministry. It contains appointments, meetings, rehearsals, family time, etc. I leave off everything that does not pertain to me directly.

Then I keep a special music schedule, including choir anthems, orchestra preludes, and special solo music for all venues. I also keep a music-selection schedule. Sometimes we get a question about how many times we have sung a particular song and on what occasion. We may get a question about the number of hymns that we are singing. I always have an answer to that question because

---

3   Sanders, *Spiritual Leadership*, 94.

of the music-selection sheet. I have been able not only to tell people but show them how we plan. This kind of organization can help us gracefully be on the offense instead of the defense when dealing with sensitive music-preference issues. More on this later...

Finally, I have a daily schedule that is updated for each week. My ministry assistant has access to my weekly schedule and can see when I have available slots for appointments. On this weekly schedule, I have built in my to-do list and standing meetings. As I complete a task, I mark it off my list.

Now, I love technology just about as much as anyone. I am first in line for apps or systems that can make my day more productive and technically savvy. Right now, I am fully automated in my scheduling, but I have not always found automation to be an effective approach for me. There have been seasons in my ministry when I found great satisfaction by taking a pen or pencil and crossing things off a paper list. Certainly, personalities and seasons can dictate which method will work best. Either way, we need a systematic approach to schedules and a willingness to live by them. Schedules, calendars, and lists help us move forward.

It is amusing that my tech and media teams were once die-hard mobile-device everything. All they brought to a meeting was their smartphone or tablet. They would make fun of me for not using mine in the same way. They read their Bibles, checked agendas, took notes, and scheduled meetings all from their phones. After some time, they wanted to get away from the "norm" of having everything on their devices and now actually bring paper and pen. I have always found that changing methods can sometimes be beneficial and keep us motivated.

In addition to a to-do list, we may benefit from having a *not-to-do* list. There are tasks within a day that, if we are not careful, can distract us from getting the more important things done—those things within the day that only we can do. There are those other tasks that we may be doing that we could give or delegate to someone else. I have made a list of things that others are doing for me. That is my not-to-do list, and it serves as a reminder for me to keep the main things the main things on my schedule. I include this list in a corner of my to-do list.

Often we have a big dream that we have been putting off. Honestly, there will never be a better time to do it than now. The first step to getting it done is putting it on the calendar. Someone may be good at writing or arranging songs and feel as if he or she has a gift in this area, but it has been hard to get beyond the task-driven nature of the workweek. The answer may be simply to schedule in a writing time. This solution may sound very simpleminded, but so few people do it. I have a very demanding ministry schedule. I am in a high-capacity, high-expectation ministry. I could be completely swallowed up by the organizational tasks that are necessary to run our ministry on a daily basis. But I have more time than I think. We must become masters of our schedule so that we can maximize our effectiveness and make the most of every possible opportunity.

Care Group Leaders— Closing the Back Door

One of the best things that I have ever discovered is the power of care groups. They were already established when I arrived at Westside. But it took me some time to realize just how vital these groups could be. Care groups have turned out to be the growth arm of our ministry.

Care groups function just like small-group Sunday school classes without the lesson. We have about twenty-six groups in our ministry. Each group has a care group leader. This leader is responsible for contacting their group at least once a week. They disperse important and timely information and act as a filter for my choir and orchestra members. They build relationships with those who are in their group and pray with their group members on a regular basis. Some groups fellowship together and even exchange gifts for birthdays and at Christmas. These groups function in a way that brings unity and care for those who participate in our shared ministry.

Each group has eight to ten members. When we gain new members, they are immediately assigned a care group. I cannot emphasize too much how valuable this practice has been for our ministry. When I began to place importance and value in the care group leaders, they began caring for and loving our people in ways that I never could.

Eventually I made our twenty-six leaders part of our music ministry leadership team. I meet with them multiple times a year and teach them leadership principles. We go through training together, Bible study, prayer, and then we discuss information critical for our ministry. They help me make decisions and work as a team. I realized that if I could get twenty-six of our members to buy into and own the direction we are headed, then we can move forward fairly quickly.

Having care groups helps decrease attrition. A care group leader notices when someone is absent, has health issues, is getting discouraged, etc. The group can then minister to the member and usually enables and/or encourages the person to stay in the choir. The leader can also inform me if there is ministry that I need to do.

This trained group of people also work as my recruiters, and they disciple their own care group members. I have even challenged our care groups to go on a mission trip together. I highly encourage putting a care-group-leader system in place. If the choir is small, the members can function as if they are one care group. If a choir has more than thirty members, I would then suggest that care-group-leader teams begin to care for and love the people in the ministry. Any music minister can be highly blessed by this organizational development.

Worship Planning

In survival mode, worship planning is a necessary evil we love to hate. In a thriving and vibrant ministry, it is a joy that we get to do! Either way, worship planning is one of those things that are required of a worship pastor. If we learn to take control of it, we can make this task an enjoyable part of our ministry.

Worship planning should never be an afterthought. It should be a priority! In my schedule, I have some time every day dedicated to worship planning. My most intense worship-planning day is on Monday. Then each day of the week, I try to work on a different aspect. For example, on Monday, I work on music selections for the worship sets for the next few weeks. We have three morning-worship venues and Sunday night services, so I have multiple sets to prepare. I like to work as far in advance as I can, but I typically get about three weeks ahead.

On Tuesdays, I may spend time doing long-range planning for special music. I consider soloists or special groups for all our venues as well as Sunday night.

Because I plan choir anthems at least four to six months in advance, I always try to review a month ahead and make any adjustments necessary to do my best rehearsal planning. On Thursdays, I try to spend a little bit of time each week listening to new music. I also use this day to work on original music that we might be writing or arranging. Because of sometimes crazy ministry demands, this planning schedule ebbs and flows at times. Since our weekend ministry is the most important thing we do, I always make worship planning the priority.

There is no magic formula for worship planning, putting together a worship set or service. However, there are things that I do to help make it as meaningful as possible. Most importantly, I rarely do worship planning alone. Our services have become too complex for me to remember everything that needs to be thought through. While I have the final say of music flow and selections, I love to have suggestions and help with this. In my case, I have my staff to help me, and we will have creative worship-planning sessions together. Before I had a music staff, I assembled a group of volunteers to help plan worship. It consisted of some of my key laypeople within my ministry, such as my pianist, organist, and other strategic personnel. This collaboration worked very well and helped produce ownership and thoughtful insight into our weekend services. It also helped with buy-in from our congregation and dispelled most, if not all, disgruntlement with any music selections.

This concept of doing ministry planning with others was foreign to me in my early years of ministry. Now I seek to do as much ministry as I can with someone else. I try to have someone with me when I go to the hospital to make a visit or when I run to the store to pick up something for the office. This practice serves as a great training opportunity; plus, it is just fun to share life with others.

Music-Selection Sheet

As I mentioned earlier, within the area of worship planning, one practice that I incorporated many years ago was the creation of a music-selection sheet. On this sheet, I place each worship service date with the music selections. Each week, I add to this sheet. Because I record the music selections for each worship service, I can easily and quickly look back to see the last time I used a particular song.

This sheet comes in extremely handy when someone asks me about the last time that we sang a particular hymn. I always have an answer to this question. Now there is a worship-planning software that helps keep track of our music and the last time we used a particular song. But I have yet to find one that is quite as helpful as the ole music-selection document that I created years ago. As of the writing of this book, our music ministry uses extensively a worship-planning software for our library, scheduling, and text scripts, but all of our staff continue to use the music-selection document.

Meetings

Meetings are necessary and beneficial within any ministry but are only as effective as the organization and execution of the meeting. As ministers of music, we will all be required to attend many meetings and also lead some. During the week, I lead a Monday morning music-and-media staff meeting. On Monday afternoon, I attend and participate in a senior-staff meeting. On Tuesday, I attend and lead a part of our ministerial staff meeting. On Wednesday, I lead a worship-planning meeting with some of our music and media staff and our senior pastor. On Thursday, I lead a technical-script meeting for all of our venues. So my week includes a total of five meetings, which I lead or heavily participate in. These meetings can be effective and beneficial only if they are led efficiently and add value to our collective effort. Nothing is more draining than a meeting that wastes time and takes away from work for kingdom growth.

When preparing to lead a meeting, we should start with an agenda. Whether we are meeting with four hundred people or with one person, an agenda is a must for maximizing our time. The agenda sets the course for the meeting and demonstrates to the person or persons whom we are meeting that we value our time and theirs—that we want the meeting to be productive. Once we have prepared a written agenda, we can plan the pace and flow of our discussions and agenda items. Preparing an agenda and planning for a meeting can take some time, but it is well worth the effort and saves time in the end.

Most meetings are nonproductive because they lack action. Discussion should lead to the identification of action items and next steps. Meetings should always empower and move the individual or group forward by assigning tasks and the next steps with due dates. Walt Disney always said, "Everyone needs deadlines. Even the beavers. They loaf around all summer, but when they are faced with the winter deadline, they work like fury. If we didn't have deadlines, we'd stagnate."[4] I think it is safe to say that everyone benefits from a deadline.

During my Monday morning music-and-media staff meeting, we always spend time evaluating the Sunday services. We celebrate the good things and then discuss the things that did not go so great—including new and different ideas that we have. We avoid talking about things that we cannot change or control. Once we have identified some things that we can improve or things that need to be added or taken away, we make assignments or task lists with dates to make the changes as quickly as possible. This evaluation has proven beneficial in my ministry.

Some personalities shy away from situations that require accountability or deadlines. In my experience, it is always a detriment if a person does not find value in implementing organization, schedules, and deadlines. These people are usually the least creative and productive people in ministry organization.

Finally, when leading a meeting, we must have sensitivity to the pace of the meeting. We need to maximize the time and the synergy of the group. If a meeting progresses too slowly from one item to the next or if it gets bogged down in a discussion of one topic, the meeting can quickly lose energy and effectiveness. Our

---

4   Walt Disney, The Walt Disney Company.

crowd barometer should always be scanning for body language and looking for signs to help decide when to move on with the agenda or when it is all right to stay put for a while longer. This crowd barometer is an art form, is not easy, and is a skill that has to be learned. We do want to be careful not to sacrifice the quality of a meeting just to save time, but we also do not want to sacrifice time if there is no need. Most people do not want to spend any more time in a meeting than is absolutely necessary. So we need to be aware of the content, pace of the content, and level of participation from the attendees to help guide us in conducting effective meetings.

The last thing I will say about meetings has to do with a start time and an end time. It is important that every meeting, rehearsal, or service that we conduct start and end on time. This is important when showing our people that we value and respect the time they have given us. I have had numerous people over the years tell me how they appreciate how diligent I am to start and end on time. When we are consistent with keeping good time, then on the occasion that we need to take more time than we originally scheduled, our ministry participants and staff members will be more willing and gracious to give us more time when we ask them to. Take note that if we take more time than originally stated in a meeting or a rehearsal, we must acknowledge that the allotted time is up and ask them for more time. Do not assume that they will just allow us to continue on without their permission.

Questions for Reflection

1. Is your current organizational structure large enough to support your desired growth for the future?
2. What kind of organizational items need to be added or streamlined to support your vision adequately?

3. Do you feel as if you have control over your schedule and your time, or do you constantly feel that you are behind because of other people's needs?

4. Are you maximizing the people within your organization to allow for growth?

Next Steps for Success

1. Establish a to-do list. Be sure to be as detailed as possible. Develop a comprehensive schedule of your week, month, and year.

2. Begin to develop well-thought-out agendas for meetings. Be sure to remember the principles of conducting a great meeting and making the most of your time.

3. Consider developing a care group system to help you grow and take care of your people. Start by communicating with a few committed people and sharing that you want them to help you move forward and grow your ministry.

12

Motivating the
People in Our Ministry

Finally, brothers, we instructed you how
to live in order to please God,
as in fact you are living. Now we ask you
and urge you in the Lord Jesus
to do this more and more.

—1 Thessalonians 4:1 (NIV)

BELIEVE IT OR not, deep down inside, most people want to be challenged. They want to be stretched. People desire to be a part of something worthwhile and bigger than themselves. This desire is why we, as leaders, have a great opportunity and responsibility on a weekly basis to challenge the people we lead to be better for the sake of Christ and His work. If we continue to do the same things in ministry in the same ways over and over again and, surprisingly, seem to be achieving the same results, then perhaps we are not challenging our people to grow and become better. It is much easier to keep the status quo. No sudden moves and nobody gets hurt! Right? But the status quo is not the abundant life through Christ that God desires for all of us.

Before we are able to help our people grow and motivate them to achieve something greater, we must first grow in the Lord and learn to lead ourselves. Leading ourselves—this is the greatest leadership challenge. But once we begin to lead and challenge ourselves, then we will be able to lead and challenge our people effectively and consistently. For me, this process is a constant work in progress and does not come without its difficulties. To be challenged means change is inevitable, and no one really likes to pay the price of change. But with resolve and the help of the Holy Spirit, we can emerge as better individuals and make a greater impact.

I'm sure that you have heard or have used these statements: "People will only give you so much of their time" or, "We can only expect a few hours from our ministry participants each week." I actually believe that these are only partially true statements and are only true if participants are not being challenged and motivated for a greater purpose. In cases where participation is limited, it is typically because the leader is trying to persuade people to do something that they are not convinced is worth their time or are not convinced will make a positive impact on the kingdom. Otherwise, my experience is that people will give a great deal of their time when they are being mentally, spiritually, emotionally, or physically challenged for a greater cause that brings meaning and purpose to their lives.

One great example of this in our ministry is *The Gainesville Christmas Festival.*

We just celebrated ten years of this grand scale Christmas production. The Gainesville Christmas Festival is a three-act, Broadway style show that is approximately two and a half hours in length. This year, we had ten performances over two weekends to over-capacity crowds. We have a cast and crew of nearly five hundred people who spend hours upon hours of time in training, rehearsing, and preparing for this gigantic, god-sized undertaking.

Besides the hundreds of people who have made professions of faith in Christ and the numerous other decisions for rededication, baptism, and membership, one of the most significant and powerful effects that come from the Christmas Festival is the unity that is present within the church family. These people do not give hundreds of hours of time each year for ten years just to put on a nice Christmas program. That in and of itself is not sufficient or worthy of all the time, energy, and sacrifice. But the fact that the Gainesville Christmas Festival has the distinct purpose of reaching people for Christ and sharing the good news of the gospel compels our church family to do what they do each year. We are always in awe as we watch the Lord take our efforts, for His namesake, and accomplish far more than we could ever accomplish on our own. Because our church family can see the hand of God at work in their lives and within our congregation during this season, our cast and crew totally discredit the idea that people will only give you a little bit of their time. On the other hand, they completely demonstrate the fact that people will give unfettered amounts of time, energy, effort, and resources when aligned with a kingdom focused purpose.

As I mentioned earlier, I recently asked our choir care group leaders to consider leading their care groups on a mission trip. Talk about a challenge. They looked at me as if I had lost my mind. Just imagine how a mission trip could change lives and make an eternal impact. Just think how much deeper the worship could be of those who have engaged the challenge of being out of their comfort zone on the mission field.

A few summers ago, I encouraged our music ministry to participate in a Bible study on worship. My desire was for them to grow deeper in their walk with the Lord and in their personal worship. As a result, I prayed that vibrant corporate worship would emerge and we would begin to see fruits of the growing discipleship. The Lord was gracious and answered my prayer.

We have seen lasting fruits and impact. This process helps move ministry from merely surviving each week to a vibrant and sweet fellowship, seeking to make a lasting impact in their world.

We need to think outside the box. How can we bring deeper meaning to the lives of the people whom we lead? How can we challenge them to think outside of themselves? How can we create a larger-than-life environment, bigger than any one person or personality?

Training

Every week, worship pastors forfeit opportunities to train and equip because we are in the throes of survival. I really believe that called men and women of God who have a love for the church will jump at the opportunities to train and be equipped if they see the need and the opportunity to do so. The fact is, many worship pastors are how I was—I just did not know what to do or how to do it.

In our ministry here, we are challenged daily to find opportunities to train and equip. In our environment, it is our only chance for success. In any environment, it is our only chance for growth. In fact, it is a biblical model for success. It's called discipleship. If we desire to have a ministry beyond survival, we must figure out a way to identify, gather, and train our leaders.

At Westside, our worship team, made up of our praise team and band, is a group of natural leaders by default. We work to put our best foot forward with our praise team singers and band members. We require a higher standard for them. They must put in extra time, and they have to sign a covenant in order to be able to participate. So naturally, I already have some great leaders and, as a result, great friends of the ministry in this group of people. I have identified my worship team as a group of leaders whom I want to invest in and train.

During each rehearsal, after singing a few songs, I often have a leadership time or a Bible study time. We are either studying the Word together or training about leadership principles together. During the early days, my leadership time included teaching stage etiquette and presentation. We talked about what to wear, how to hold a microphone, how to be comfortable on the platform, how to communicate a song, etc. Now we can go deeper in our leadership training. I talk to them as if they are fellow staff members (with certain restrictions, of course). I train them in the inner workings and expectations of our ministry. I also get their input on direction and strategy. They *love* this and appreciate that I invest in them and seek their opinion in return. As a result, they become my ambasadors, my eyes and ears, and they all really care about the overall impact and quality of our music and worship ministry. These leaders are a significant contribution to the reason that we have moved from a ministry of just survival to a ministry of strength, impact, and success.

My next identified group of leaders are the twenty-six Choir Care Group leaders I mentioned in chapter 11. Each care group leader is responsible for eight to ten persons within our choir. I meet with this group regularly on Sunday nights. I communicate differently to this group than to my worship team. I want my care group leaders to know the ins and outs of our ministry so they can be the champions of my vision among our people. I constantly articulate our vision to this group. We go through leadership training lessons, and then we discuss ministry information. Every month, I give them a report of all our ministry's financial account information, future major purchases, ideas, goals, etc. Then I always give them an opportunity to speak. I tell them that I want to hear from them. I always try to implement things that they suggest if it is possible.

They are very creative, and they care about the choir and orchestra. They have helped me dodge some bullets, and this group has certainly created an environment of creativity and success. I always keep tight guidelines with our discussion and make sure that I lead them, but there is a sense of free flow in communication. I have trained them about how to deal with complaints and concerns that they hear voiced about our ministry and some of our decisions.

They know how to respond and answer questions on my behalf. This group of leaders has become a growth agent and a strength for sustaining a creative, growing, and vibrant ministry. The awesome thing that has transpired is that these leaders in whom I am investing are investing in others. For instance, our care group leaders teach the leadership lessons to the members of their group. This is leadership multiplication at its finest. If we want to build an impactful ministry that reaches beyond the music on Sunday mornings, we must systematically train our people. Use rehearsal times and regular meetings. Do not waste any time. Kingdom work is at stake. Think beyond the music.

Here is a note of caution for all of us. People are keenly aware of what level their leaders are leading from and what they are willing to do to lead and love well. If we are not yet known for our high standards, then we may need to start small. We cannot challenge our people further than we are capable of going ourselves. They will not respond favorably. We may want to begin by doing a Bible study on worship together or begin with a leadership lesson from time to time. Our system of training and challenge has taken years to develop, with plenty of baby steps. But also, do not hold back. If our people are ready for a challenge and we have established our leadership and gained their trust, then I suggest we go big. Challenge them in significant ways and see what the Lord does!

Questions for Reflection

1. In what ways are you challenging and stretching yourself personally?
2. How have you grown spiritually and in ministry over the past six months?
3. Are you in a position to motivate your people to grow?
4. Do people find value in your ministry, or is it hard to get them connected?

Next Steps for Success

1. Begin with yourself. Be sure that you are growing and developing your own life and ministry. Challenge yourself.
2. Seek ways to motivate the people in your ministry. Plan a mission trip, lead a Bible study, develop a leadership lesson.
3. Work to develop a system of challenge and an environment of learning.

13

Communicating for Success

Communication—the human connection—
is the key to personal and career success.

—Paul J. Meyer[1]

INFORMATION EMPOWERS PEOPLE. It gives them the ability to make good decisions. It helps them feel that they are valued. Communication is one of our greatest assets as we move from survival to success. The right kind of communication to the right people at the right time can make a definitive difference about how they will respond.

Many leaders do not like giving people information. For some reason, it makes them feel less in charge or afraid that they have given their edge away. It is true that we must have discernment about the information we need and ought to share. When it comes to information about my ministry, I have learned that, more often than not, the more information that I can give, the better. I disseminate information in layers. My first layer of communication is to my music and media staff. They know almost everything. Notice I said *almost*. I decide with my music staff what

---

1 Paul J. Meyer, source unknown.

information is shared with my lay leaders when I meet with them once a month. Then I, along with my lay leadership group, decide what and when to share with the ministry at large. Keep in mind that this is my general principle of information dissemination and not my everyday model. It would be impractical to have to run everything by a group of people every day.

I use this tier model when communicating ideas, new projects, goals, and major emphases. The reason I do this information sharing is because I want to make sure that I am not working unilaterally. Meaning, I am not making all the decisions from my office and not giving any thought to how a decision will be received or how it will affect the persons we are equipping to do the work of ministry. Appropriately shared information also creates a sense of ownership or buy-in to a new goal or project. Next, it helps add value to people. When dealing with normal, everyday issues or making a decision on everyday systematic things, I always ask myself, "Who else do I get to tell?" I have even printed this question on a piece of paper and taped it to my door.

For instance, we offer childcare for our rehearsals. During some parts of the season, it is necessary for us to cancel a rehearsal. Well, naturally, I communicate a canceled rehearsal to my rehearsal participants; but on a few occasions, I have forgotten to communicate with the children's ministry, and they have scheduled childcare workers. Then there is great frustration because I forgot to let the right people know. Not only did it mess up people's schedules, but it also wasted money. This lack of communication is just a small and simple example, but the same principle applies to all levels of circumstances.

Most relationship issues are caused by a lack of communication. Without the correct information, most people will make assumptions about decisions if they are left to make their own conclusions. Because people tend to think the worst first, lack of communication can breed unnecessary tension and lack of understanding. One of the reasons it may seem that we can never move forward in our ministry is that we are constantly "putting out fires." We need to move from being a "firefighter" to being a "fire preventer." Being proactive in our information sharing will drastically reduce the potential for frustrations and lack of understanding. We imagine that, surely, people know that all our decisions are pure of heart and for their best interests, right? *Wrong!* We know our intentions, but when others do not know, they are left to interpret our decisions and leadership through the lens of their own perspective. Communication can dispel rumors and wrong assumptions. The right information at the right time has the power to build trust and consistency. People like to know where they are going, and more importantly, they like to know why they are going there.

Unless it is a unique and controlled environment, I never ask a group of people, "What do you want to do?" "What do you guys want to talk about?" or "What is your vision?" In my opinion, this is a leadership *no-no*. If we begin meetings or times of communication this way, we need to stop. There will be an appropriate time for discussion and questions, but people want to be led. They need to know that we have a plan and are not just shooting from the hip. Always have a plan. Be ready to guide and lead. Then form questions to help guide the group to think and affirm our leadership or help steer us otherwise. Just note, we have been called to lead; and if we have loved and served our people well with consistency and wisdom, then they will certainly want to hear and understand our direction of leadership.

When communicating anything, the why is the first thing that needs to be explained.

For instance, about three years ago, our ministry was faced with a major issue. We were growing beyond our facility's capacity. Our choir room, choir loft, and stage were very quickly getting too small to rehearse the choirs for our two worship services together. With no money and no room to expand, I began to pray and research what we could do. I asked my staff; we brainstormed with our lay music leadership. I finally came to the conclusion that we would have to reconfigure our Wednesday night rehearsals in order to continue to grow.

With the addition of some chairs in our choir room, I knew that we could sustain a little bit more growth. However, we could only seat a few over ninety in our choir loft. We were filling that up, and I had already pulled the praise team out of the loft. The choir family loved the *big* feel, and they did not mind sitting close together. It was for a good cause, and they could see that we were growing. However, I knew that if I did not make a growth decision soon, their excitement and willingness to endure would be short-lived.

I made the decision to begin the year with the choir sitting in chairs on the floor of the worship center facing the stage with the orchestra sitting behind me. With the worship center seating, we could configure the rehearsal space and add as many chairs as needed. So after communicating with our staff, leadership, and my pastor, we decided to make this risky move. I collaborated with as many leaders as I could before I made this decision. I sought their wisdom and heard their suggestions.

I paid careful attention to the detail of the setup. I made signs for the sections and had them elevated on poles so that they could easily be seen. I spent a lot of time making sure the sections were miced properly so that the choir would be able to hear. My staff helped me walk through every detail of the evening from the perspective of a choir member to make sure that we were creating an exceptional first-time experience in a new environment.

As choir members walked through the doors, we had section leaders ready to guide them to the right seats. There were puzzled looks on the faces of the people, and they knew we were up to something interesting.

I started rehearsal by singing a few songs so that they could get used to the environment. Then after our opening prayer, I asked people to sit down. I began to tell them the story and gave them a little bit of statistical information about how we had grown. I told them that in order to sustain current growth and continue to grow, we had to do something. I was telling them the why. Then I was careful to explain that even though we knew it would be a little weird at first and that we would trade off some of our conveniences of being in an ideal configuration in the choir loft, it was more important to make room for more people.

I explained that we had thought of different scenarios, had discussed this change extensively, and had prayed at length. I even had our senior pastor present at that rehearsal so that he could give extra weight and communication concerning the importance of our decision.

As I finished my communication about this huge new change for all of us, our choir treasurer came up and whispered the attendance in my ear. On that very night, we had more in choir than we had ever had and more than we would have been able to fit in the previous loft configuration. So the change proved its necessity that night. Our choir and orchestra met the why, how, and when with great enthusiasm. To this very day, we have continued to grow in this now *normal* configuration.

The careful communication and execution of this major shift in our weekly environment helped to make this change in our shared ministry a success. Had I made this decision without communicating to anyone, even with the necessity of the move, things could have taken a turn for the negative very quickly.

When I first began my ministry at Westside, I was quite the young whippersnapper. I understood that in order to gain followership and begin to grow a ministry, I would have to build trust. I knew that one of the best ways to gain trust is through communicating a vision and a strategy. My wife suggested that

I create a booklet of important information and promote the idea that we were going to have the most important choir and orchestra rehearsal of the year, just so we could peak interest and foster a high attendance. Well, I took my wife's wise suggestion and did just that. I communicated that we would have "the most important choir and orchestra rehearsal of the year." Again, I was sure to pay attention to the details to ensure that this rehearsal would be a high-quality experience. I created a very detailed multipage booklet that explained our vision, goals, objectives, and strategy. I also included a needs-and-wants list, as well as philosophies of ministry. I took the entire rehearsal time to go through the booklet and cast my vision to the members of my ministry. I took the time to explain the why of every initiative.

We have had this tradition ever since, and it is one of the highlights of our year. In fact, it has grown to something we call *vision week*. This week is filled with leadership training, ministry opportunities, a vision-casting night, worship, and then we conclude the week with a formal banquet. We do it a little different each year, and I will often invite guest speakers and clinicians to help teach and train us in different areas of our ministry. The information that is shared during this week and particularly on "the most important choir practice of the year" is our guiding map for the year and explains our direction, as well as how we plan to spend our money. This small effort is a "fire-prevention" system. It communicates where we are going and what our people can expect to experience during the year.

Throughout the year, I revisit initiatives from our booklet as we get ready to engage them. This review always helps refresh the vision and gets people realigned behind our direction because they are reminded of why we are doing what we are doing. Naturally, there are times when we have a change of direction, or when circumstances warrant us to shift some goals and needs. But because I have already communicated an in-depth strategy, a level of trust has already been established. For the most part, simple communication of a change, along with an explanation of the why, yields full support and understanding from our ministry participants.

Here are the different forms of communication that we use:

1. *Weekly e-mail.* I send out one e-mail per week to our entire ministry. Everyone knows that it is coming, and I use it to send encouragement, instructions, and reminders.

2. *Worship ministry website.* We communicate heavily through our own ministry website. We update weekly information so that people will visit the site regularly. Not only do we post information, but we provide additional tools for worship preparation, such as a stream of our choir music so that our choir and orchestra can listen to upcoming music. We place ministry photos, links, lessons, and various other things on this site.

3. *Vision week.* This week is full of communication and leadership training and also includes our "most important choir and orchestra rehearsal of the year."

4. *Meetings.* I have meetings on a regular basis to maintain a systematic approach to communication and leadership training.

5. *Social media.* I use social media often to build excitement, intrigue, and anticipation. I rarely use it for recruiting or information disbursement.

Fire Prevention vs. Firefighting

I learned this concept from one of my mentors, Dr. Bailey, and I have referred to it earlier. He used to tell me to learn to think ahead in order to prevent a crises or a "fire." He taught me that most people wait before dealing with conflict and allow a "fire" to start and then try to put it out instead of working on the offense to make sure conflict does not flare up. Over the years, I have experienced the truth of this wisdom, and I have learned that fire prevention is an act of love and thoughtfulness. If we are dealing with serious issues in our ministry or we see that something might cause a conflict, we must do the hard work up-front by going to the people involved in the conflict to get things resoved so that there are no mishaps.

One of the greatest sources of conflict is lack of communication or miscommunication. Our staff helps solve this issue in our organization by asking in our meetings the question mentioned earlier: Who else needs to know? This simple phrase, which we often speak to one another when we are finalizing details for an event or a major focus or project, serves as a reminder for all involved to think through whom we need to communicate with. It is an intentional process to foster good communication. In our music and media ministries, I have tweaked this question a little and reworded it: Who else do I get to tell? This question suggests another step beyond just basic communication. It calls for additional thinking on the part of our staff and has a more exciting ring. This process may sound too simple and cheesy, but we have adopted this idea and find it very beneficial. All my staff members have a printout of this question posted somewhere in a visible place in their offices or studios.

I often talk to my staff about fire prevention, training them to think ahead about possible questions that could be asked or possible pitfalls in certain ideas and programs. This concept is a must for creative teams who plan weekend services and need to get many people on the same page to coordinate the execution of a worship service.

Questions for Reflection

1. Are you quick to communicate information, or do you tend to hold on to it?
2. Are you afraid to share information? If so, why?
3. What is your systematic approach to communication in your ministry?
4. Are you a firefighter or a fire preventer?

Next Steps for Success

1. Map out on paper your regular communication plan.
2. Start thinking in terms of, Who do I get to tell?
3. Start communicating clear, concise, and helpful information. Do not be afraid to give your information and plans away.

Successful Environments of Growth and Change

Growth itself is the only moral end.

—John Dewey[1]

CHANGE IS INEVITABLE. Since God designed a world that is constantly changing, He must have intended for us to see change as a necessary and helpful process in which to live life to the fullest. I see change as a built-in accountability for progression of life as a believer and our growing and changing relationship with the Father.

We often shy away from change, but that resistant does us no good. We will eventually be forced to change whether we want to or not. Sometimes we can be too aggressive and abuse or manipulate the force of change. I feel that God has given us the ability to develop successful habits and willingness about change that makes it an enriching and kingdom-benefiting factor in our lives and ministry. Since we know we will be changing,

---

1   John Dewey, wisdoquotes.com, accessed, September 2013.

I have identified some principles that have helped me manage change successfully.

Producing Successful Change in a New Environment

At some time in our ministry we will be known as "the new guy." When immediately thrust into a leadership role as the new guy, it is often difficult to know what to do. How do we produce change when we are the new kid on the block? There are a thousand answers to this question. Ultimately, we will need to trust the Lord for guidance when trying to make the best decisions about bringing needed change in a new environment. I am going to share some insights from my own perspective and experiences over the years in the hope that there may be some experiences that can help someone else.

Understand Your Job Description

Anyone who was not presented a job description before accepting a position with a new church or organization may have made a major mistake. It may be better to stop reading this book right now and find out immediately how to get a job description for the position. It is extremely important that we know the expectations and boundaries of our position and have them in writing so that we can refer back to them occasionally. These expectations can act as our accountability guide and give us clues as to what level we are expected to perform. It is our responsibility to know and understand what is expected of us. If we do not do this and then fail to meet expectations, it will most likely be our fault. I have always sought ways to raise the standard of my job description. The questions that we should ask ourselves are, How will this job description have to be changed when they are considering who will take my place? How will we raise the expectations of our organization as it pertains to our ministry position?

Learn the Context

Every church or organization has a context of operation. There are always reasons, good or bad, why things are done the way are. There are emotions and hard work attached to processes and organizations. If we are going to be successful at making needed changes, we are going to have to learn the context in which our ministry or organization exists and operates. This research can be accomplished by asking well-thought-out questions about the processes and environment where we are. We need to talk to as many people as possible and learn as much as we can quickly.

I have always found history fascinating. I like to read the history of anything. My family and I are big Walt Disney World fans. We love everything about it. But the reason I love it the most is the history and the stories that preceded the family attractions and resorts that we enjoy now. Walt Disney World has not always been what it is today. It had beginnings, trials, compromises, decisions, etc. There is a story attached to everything! We make a mistake if we short-circuit our effort to learn all we can about a new place of ministry. The history and context will give us a new level of appreciation and insight when seeking to lead forward.

Learn the Leader

If we want to produce change in a new environment, we will need to learn how our pastor/leader thinks, processes information, and can be influenced. High-capacity leaders typically move at a very fast pace and do not like their time taken by unnecessary details and stories. We have to learn how our leader likes to receive information and make that our method of delivery. We will be able to accomplish more with our leaders' approval if we learn how to communicate with them effectively.

I arrived at my current church in May of 2006. I told the search committee that I had a heart and a vision for a large community Christmas production. They were enthusiastic about some of my thoughts but were quick to tell me about the history of the church's historic community Easter pageant and how much our pastor intended on bringing this back once there was a new worship pastor in place. In initial talks with the senior pastor, he also shared his vision to reinstate the beloved Easter pageant. I knew that the Lord was calling me to our ministry position at Westside, but I also knew that my vision was for a large Christmas event, so I figured that it would work out.

On day one, I began asking worship ministry leadership to tell me about their vision for bringing back the Easter pageant. One by one, they told me how they were burned out from the Easter pageant but that our senior pastor really wanted it back. The more I talked to people to learn the context of the Easter pageant, the more I realized that no one who would be responsible for making it happen really had a passion or a vision for it—but they all had the desire to champion the vision of their senior pastor. This was a big clue for me! I knew that I could most likely get the music and worship ministry leadership to buy into the Christmas vision fairly easily, but if I wanted to fulfill my vision for Christmas, I would have to have my senior pastor on board.

Every time I met with my senior pastor, I brought up my thoughts for Christmas. He was very encouraging and listened with enthusiasm, but then in the next breath, he would ask me about the progress on Easter and getting that reestablished. I knew we could not do both Easter and Christmas and see my vision for a large-scale Christmas production have the time and resources to mature. I went home one day after a meeting with the senior pastor and told my wife, Carolyn, that if we were ever going to see our vision to do a large Christmas event come to reality, we would have to do it *this* Christmas, and it would have to be a success. I knew that I needed to give my pastor a new experience in order for him to understand what I wanted to do.

Now, let me be clear. Even though I was a twenty-five-year-old whippersnapper coming into a large ministry with high expectations, my pastor was supportive of me from day one. It was understandable that he would want to build on a past positive experience—in this case, the Easter pageant. One day in early June of that first year, I was talking with my pastor about Christmas when he again brought up the question about my plans for Easter. So I told him, "Yes, I'm working on it." I actually did my homework to see what my options were. Meanwhile, I set sail full steam ahead to produce our Christmas show within about five and a half months. Well, we poured everything we could into that first year. We met with a lot of people and cast a lot of vision, and by the grace of God, we had a successful first annual Gainesville Christmas Festival.

The week after we finished the festival, my pastor took me to lunch. We received our appetizer, and then he looked at me, took a deep breath, and said, "All right, you have my attention." He was able to understand the vision for Christmas and how it could benefit us in our city. But he also came to the realization that we could not do both the Christmas festival and the Easter pageant. So he left the decision up to me and gave me his full support.

This year, we will produce the tenth annual Gainesville Christmas Festival with ten performances over two weekends and will welcome thousands of guests on our campus. Here is the point to this story: I learned what was important to my pastor, listened to him, and respected the history of why he felt the way he did about Easter. Then I was able to build trust and respect from my pastor and the people in my ministry so that I could bring change in my new environment.

Make Decisions Quickly That Add Value Immediately

I have known ministers who have a rule that they will wait six months to a year before they attempt to change anything! I have never thought that this delay is a good idea. Change is inevitable, so we may want to take some steps to build trust and momentum as quickly as possible while everyone's tolerance level is high. We have all probably heard this called the *honeymoon period*. No matter what we call it, the first few months naturally give us a period of opportunity and advantage, but it is important to use the time carefully and wisely.

When coming into a new environment, visionary leaders will notice right away things that they would like to change or spruce up. A new person has the advantage of fresh eyes to see things that everyone else cannot see anymore, such as a cluttered space, a spotty carpet, or an old paint job. We can use our fresh eyes to our advantage to build some excitement. When I first came to our church, the chairs in the choir room were hard metal folding chairs, mixed with old choir chairs from the previous church location. It made the very nice and fairly new choir room look unintentional and outdated. I found out that we had about 120 extra chairs for the worship center that were not being used. So I had the mismatched chairs replaced with all matching padded chairs. The folding chairs were put into storage, and the old choir chairs were donated to a new church plant across town. When the choir members walked into the choir room the following Wednesday night, they could not believe their eyes. Someone even said, "What did we do to deserve nice matching chairs?" This change cost nothing and added value to the room and the people.

Over the next few weeks, we cleaned, organized, painted, and polished. With each visible noninvasive change, we built anticipation, excitement, and a culture of change. I was able to make these quick little tweaks that made a major impact and paved the way for years of more significant change and growth. Besides cosmetic changes, we can also make slight shifts in organizational patterns that will immediately add value.

The first few weeks and months are critical in developing our leadership among the people. With quick decisive "moves" that were not heavy in their consequences but added value to the organization, I was able to establish that I have a plan and thoughtful intentions for my leadership. This perception is very important to establish right away, and these kinds of changes are a great way to do it.

Make Cautious, Invasive Decisions

Certainly, there are more significant ministry decisions that need to be made that we will see right away when coming into a new ministry environment. I caution the leader who comes in full force ready to make tough, invasive changes right away. Unless it is a moral or integrity issue, which should be dealt with biblically and immediately, large or sacred organizational changes should be approached carefully and in a timely way. Good or bad, someone has paid a price for the ministry that we are stepping into. So when changes that will require some paradigm shifts in thinking or practice need to be made, we will need to take some time to consider the people who will be affected by the changes.

I have seen many staff members and pastors walk into a church and completely change times, format, mandate, vision, mission, and/or organizational structure within weeks or months of arriving. I cannot recall ever seeing that scenario having a happy ending. In most cases, invasive changes will need to be considered with collective wisdom from a group of people. We may ultimately have to make the decision and then be the sole person responsible for the outcome, but we will be better prepared to manage the challenges of the results of the decisions if we have others walking with us and helping us see multiple perspectives.

Successful Spaces

In our American culture, our space to do life is extremely important. I am a nester. The look and feel of our home is very important to me. I need my home to be clean and well put together for me to feel at rest. My wife just cares about the function of space and the cleanliness. The decor doesn't mean that much to her. No matter our personality, the space environment plays a role on how we feel and function when in that space. We have unspoken standards within our society when it comes to spaces. When we go into a hospital, doctor's office, grocery store, or department store, we expect and even hunt for places that are clean, up-to-date, and make us feel warm and as if everything is in order. We cannot minister to a culture of people with these standards, not adhere to them within our ministries, and then expect to maximize our ministry effectiveness.

Musicians are creative people, and creative people need creative spaces. Not only are we creative, but also the people whom we lead are creative and need a space to be the best at their art. Whatever our space is, how big or how small, we need to make it as nice as it can possibly be.

When I first came to Westside, I walked into a five-year-old facility. The choir room had become the catchall place. Storage rooms were stuffed to the max with old equipment, broken furniture, file cabinets—you name it, it was in there. Every corner of the choir room had been claimed by a different ministry, and there were file cabinets crammed full of stuff. I already mentioned the mismatched chairs in the center of the room for choir members. It appeared that the music ministry had become neglected in terms of leadership and had diminished significantly.

I knew that if I wanted to have a successful ministry, I would need a good space from which to work and build.

Space was my first and most important mission in my first few months at Westside. I had to create an environment that added value to my ministry and was going to give our people a great place to make great music. I started by cleaning out and throwing things away. My wife came to church and helped me! It took us a few weeks, but we finally got to a clean space. Once that was accomplished, I made sure that the floors were shiny and clean and that the room smelled clean. Then I made sure that the chairs matched and it looked like a room with intention and purpose. Besides some cleaning supplies, I do not think my cleaning spree cost any money at all. I used the resources that we had and just created a clean, neat, and purposeful environment. With the space clean and functional, I eventually and gradually made further improvements that gave it meaning and detail. For instance, we updated the media and technology in the room to help support the priorities and philosophy of our ministry. Then we installed a small welcome center and made sure that we were ready to receive guests.

Here are some other things that we have included in the space over the years:

- Banners and large prints on the walls. These can be inspiring and make a space feel warm as long as they are not tacky or outdated.
- Paint. Not only does this help a space look fresh but smell fresh too. Never underestimate the power of a fresh coat of paint.
- Lighting. I cannot stress how important the right kind of lighting is. If possible, have lighting that can be controlled, such as recessed, incandescent lighting. Also, feature lighting is always a nice touch.

- Scrolling announcements. These are a nice detailed touch that can add intentionality and function to a space. I recommend having this as a feature, if possible.
- Attendance-check-in computer stations. These are not necessary in most spaces but, for some, can be a valuable tool to help keep accurate attendance records.
- Signage. Do not underestimate the value of proper signage.

Regardless of the size of ministry, we can create an intentional, clean, and fresh space to build an environment that fosters growth and vitality. If rehearsal is in the choir loft or worship center, then we probably already have an intentional space that will work. Also, we need to make sure to bring in the necessary items that are needed to make that space work as a rehearsal space. When we rehearse in our worship center, we always wheel in our welcome center, skirted tables for music books and name tags, as well as our computer stations for check-in. We take the extra time to make it as intentional as possible. I have also, on occasion, set up banners on stands just to bring some energy to the environment. Be creative. We should think for our people and work hard to create a space that fosters growth!

Besides the physical environment, there is a mental environment where we grow and change mind-sets, attitudes, and move people toward change. We need to be creative to think of things that can be done on a regular basis to help create this kind of environment.

Reading for Success

One of the many things I have learned over the recent years is the benefit of being a part of a ministry that is constantly seeking new things to read, which will engage conversation and spur creativity.

It does not matter how big or small the church or how simple or complex our ministry, we can learn much by reading.

Why read? "Read to refill the wells of inspiration."[2] We read to sharpen our skills, to become wiser, but most importantly, we read to glorify God. We do not need to read only the Bible to glorify God. Yes, the Bible is the source of life and is the way to know more about God. But reading other things—about leadership, technology, history—these can all benefit and stir up inspiration within us. "The reader should read, too, to acquire new information, to keep current with the time, to be well informed in his or her field of expertise."[3]

I subscribe to as many worship leadership, church administration, and tech magazines as I possibly can. I even like getting the catalogs that have church furniture and furnishings in them. Magazines have become my dream literature. I read the articles and look at the ads. I circle things that appeal to me or give me an idea. I write down brand names, topics, locations, people's names, just to have something to discuss or think through in the future. Also, because of my heart for leadership, my bookshelves are full of leadership books (and not just by Christian authors).

My family and I are Disney junkies, and I have been bitten badly by Disney magic. I have several Disney leadership books that explain the hows and whys of the Walt Disney Company. I cannot tell you how many principles I have adapted from those books. Here is my point: reading and gathering information should be at the top of our priority list when working to move from survival to success. Over the years, I have encouraged or recommended books for people in our ministry to read. I may use the points in a book to help support ideas on worship and

---

2   Harold J. Ockenga, Christianity Today, 4 March 1966, 36.

3   Sanders, *Spiritual Leadership, 103.*

leadership. This focus on reading is a great way to foster an environment of thinking and personal growth and change.

I have recently met many people who absolutely do not like to read. But reading is a gateway to growth. "Wesley told the younger ministers of the Methodist societies to read or get out of the ministry."[4]

I was not much of a reader in my younger days, and I did not know what I was missing. Being challenged to read stirs up a hunger to read more. "Most people who decide to grow personally find their first mentors in the pages of books."[5] Here are some ways that I continue growing through my reading. First, I always try to read a book with someone. I have often offered to buy a book for someone else if he or she is willing to read and discuss it with me. For someone who does not like to read, this plan will encourage the start of a reading journey. Next, I use various leadership groups to read a book together. We commit to a chapter a week and build in time in our meetings to discuss the book.

We have done this very thing in our ministerial staff meetings, and I have often led my music staff through reading a book. Not only does this group reading fuel our desire to gain knowledge by reading, but it also encourages others on our teams who are not readers.

For those who are the only staff member in the church or ministry, some laypersons will probably be willing to form a reading group. If we have a small choir, we can ask all of them to read a leadership book or a book on worship then take ten minutes each week in rehearsal to discuss a chapter or section of the book. But be careful! We can waste our time reading junk. We

---

4   Ibid., 102.
5   John C. Maxwell, *The 15 Invaluable Laws of Growth: Live Them and Reach Your Potential*, Reprint ed. (Nashville: Center Street, 2014), 212.

need to read material that we can learn from and apply. We want to be intentional about what we read, especially when sharing a book with another person or group of people. Understand that if we try to get a large group to read, not all of them will see the value in it. Do not be discouraged. Do not try to force reading on anyone.

My former pastor, Dr. Gary Crawford, is one of the most intentional men I have ever met. One year in a staff-planning week, he gave us some of his personal criteria for his intentional reading. I asked him for permission to share what he taught us. When reading a book, he suggested the following:

1. Know the author. Read about him and understand what perspective he may be writing from.
2. Always read the introduction, foreword, preface, and dedications.
3. Date the book when you start reading and then again when you finish. Also make a note about where you are when you begin reading.
4. Create symbols to mark the book:

   - ! = I agree, good point.
   - i = Insight.
   - ? = I question this point or have a question about this idea.
   - @ = Apply this thought or principle.
   - R = Further reading is required.
   - I = This could make a good illustration.

5. Schedule any action items that need to come from your reading.
6. Journal what you have learned or think about what you are reading.

We can use these symbols if we are reading a book. However, when reading scripture, we might want to go a little further and ask ourselves some questions to help us understand what is being said. When reading scripture, ask these few questions:

1. Are there any *promises* to claim?
2. Can you give *thanksgiving* for what the scripture is saying to you?
3. Are there sins to *confess*?
4. Are there *examples* to follow?
5. Are there *commands* to obey?
6. Are there *insights* to apply?

I believe that these are some very practical ideas to help us process and get the most out of what we read. Once we get into the habit of reading, we will be able to read multiple books at one time with ease. Reading will become a part of who we are and a definitive game changer in life and ministry.

Writing for Success

It may not be obvious how writing anything can help foster an environment of growth and change. Writing is a discipline of the mind and an expression of the heart. If no one else can benefit from our writing, we can! One of the most basic forms of writing is journaling, and it is a good place to start. We need a nice journal to record thoughts, stories, insights, and plans. I have several different journals, all with different kinds of information.

I have a journal to write thoughts and ideas that pertain to ministry, and I have one for personal and family thoughts, feelings, and plans. I try to write as much as possible. I write with the idea that one day someone will read these journals. I want for whoever reads them to be able to know me and gain insight from my experiences. Many of my entries are prayers. However, most are my thoughts, ideas, feelings, and future plans.

Next, I suggest that we begin writing teachable lessons from what we read. When reading, we should be thinking, *How can I transfer this information to someone else?* We can start with writing a teachable page from a chapter of a book we are reading. In what ways am I being challenged by what the author has written? I write down the key principles from a book that could be insightful to share with others or for my own review. This practice can slow down our reading, but it can certainly propel our preparation and opportunities for leading others. Writing, like reading, is a discipline. It can be hard and time-consuming. We must determine to write with purpose and meaning.

Recently, I have had conversations with several people who are thinking about writing a book. I am in the midst of my own writing journey. I do not have much wisdom to share about this process, but what I do know is that I have always wanted to write a book. But I was never compelled to write, until now. All the authors whom I talked to over the years told me that writing is something we have to be called and compelled to do; otherwise, we will not finish the work. I took that to heart and decided that I would wait until the Lord compelled me. So far, my experience has been one of learning and fun. Writing has been in my heart and in my mind. Writing is not easy for me, so I have had to make it a discipline.

We do not have to write a grand novel, just write something. Our thoughts are certainly worthwhile and can be useful to someone at sometime in the future.

Teaching for Success

Teaching will become a natural outflow of our learning. The biggest issue I have had over the years is gathering material to teach or deciding what to teach. First, I tackled the issue of gathering material. Most material that I teach comes from things I am reading. When reading, I constantly look for things that I can teach. I regularly take time out of our rehearsals to teach a concept about worship, music, leadership, or the church in general. I am not able to do this often, but on ocassion, I have taught a Bible study on worship. This effort was very effective in helping build the right environment and mind-set of change and discipleship.

We should be teaching more than just music. We have a captive audience, and our ministry is potentially filled with spiritual leaders. We have a prime opportunity to invest in their lives and help our people grow in their walk with the Lord, their mind-set of church, and the worship of God. We also have a responsiblity to use the opportunity to develop leaders with our teaching. We should never pass up an opportunity to teach!

My last word on teaching will be one to all of us personally. If we are not learning, we will not be teaching. If we are not teaching, we are not completing the learning process. First, *never stop learning*. If we stop learning, we might as well pack up and go home. But I also know that we never truly learn something until we teach it. Teaching is learning, and learning is teaching. They go hand in hand. Teaching is as beneficial to us as it is for those who are receiveing the instruction. In fact, it may be more beneficial for us.

Successful Growth

I know that we would all like to see our ministry and church grow. The music ministry, generally speaking, cannot grow beyond a certain percentage of our congregation size. While there are other forms of growth besides numeric growth, adding people to our organization should be a priority. After all, we exist to reach people.

Environments of growth and change must be viewed holistically. There is no organization that has only a single phase of growth. Instead, healthy and growing ministries experience multiple phases of ministry life.

In his book *Axiom*, Bill Hybels spends a chapter discussing church ministry seasons. Here are the different seasons that he identifies:[6]

1. Season of growth
2. Season of consolidation
3. Season of transition
4. Season of malaise
5. Season of reinvention

Although this list is talking about overall church ministry seasons, I have taught his material numerous times to our music and worship ministry participants and leadership. As we have gone through these seasons within our church, we are now beginning to realize what these seasons look and feel like within our particular ministry. Here is what we have identified.

---

6   Bill Hybels, *Ax-i-om (Ak-see-uhm): Powerful Leadership Proverbs* (Grand Rapids, Mich.: Zondervan, 2008), 24.

Season of Growth or Addition

This season is exciting and energetic. Attendance is strong, and we are adding people to our ministry on a regular basis.

- Leaders will want to play off the energy that we are feeling during the rehearsals.
- Encourage ministry leaders each week to invite people to be a part of our ministry.
- Understand that this season will not last forever, and we will need to gain as much momentum as possible.
- Be sure to revisit the basics of ministry each week so that newcomers can become aware of expectations, and current members can be reminded of the expectations.

Season of Organization and Training

This season is necessary if we are to see lasting growth. It will need to be handled with strong leadership and focus. Our people will be more responsive to the changes that help support a season of growth.

- Identify this phase to our people. Help them know that it is necessary for lasting change.
- Work on long-range plans during this season. Provide heavy leadership training.
- Work through our systematic organizational and communication system with a fine-tooth comb.
- Be sure to communicate heavily with our ministry participants and bring them along with us.
- Growth will always force organizational changes, so be sure not to ride the growth wave too long before beginning to make some changes where necessary.

Season of Rest

Rest is a necessary season and a biblical one. This season often occurs after a major church transition, a busy/hectic time, or after a season of growth and reorganization. This is a time when we can just focus on the basics of ministry and do them well.

- Update our ministry priorities and make sure that we are keeping the main things the main things.
- Love on our ministry participants well. Help them have times of rest by giving time back to them. Perhaps end rehearsal early or have some times of fellowship just to enjoy one another.
- Before exiting this phase, identify which phase we feel is coming next and begin to walk our leadership and our members through necessary steps for the next season.
- Do not plan anything unnecessary on the ministry calendar. Take some time just to breathe and get reenergized.

Season of Discovery

This is time when we get to reinvent ourselves and our ministry ideas. We can start with a clean slate and begin to rethink some of our processes and methods.

- This is a necessary season to maintain freshness and relevant processes. Be sure to use this time wisely.
- Gather people to help dream about the future and what our next ministry steps need to be to move forward.
- This is a season when the Lord may really want to reveal new ways that we can make kingdom impact, so stay prayed up and sensitive to what the Lord is doing around us.

These seasons are not in any particular order, and a combination of different seasons can be obvious at any given time. All these seasons, working together, bring about a holistic environment of growth and change. Every season is necessary and helps prepare for the next. Sometimes we have to work hard to identify properly the season that we are in and anticipate the next. Communicating for growth is one of the most critical things that we can do.

When experiencing a season of growth, enjoy it! Know that it will not last forever and that it comes with a price. When the dust settles, we will have to do some organizational, environmental, and philosophical changes in order to maintain and keep up with the growth. This follow-up is the hardest part, but it is necessary for continued and sustained growth and to keep us on a track of success. Growth without any intentional change will only lead to burnout, frustration, and missed opportunities. If no change happens with our growth, we will immediately find ourselves back in survival mode, just doing what it takes to get by for the day.

Environments, both physical and philosophical, help foster a ministry of success. Without the proper environment, we have very little chance of moving forward. When we find ourselves in an environment that is less than ideal, we must be the ones to make the changes necessary; we cannot depend on someone else. We must make the most of what we have! Let us be good stewards of where God has placed us and the resources that He has given us.

Questions for Reflection

1. What kind of things can I do to add value to my organization immediately?

2. What decisions or changes do I need to approach cautiously?

3. Are the spaces that we use on a weekly basis conducive to our best work?

4. What skills or disciplines do I need to gain to help me grow as a leader?

5. What season of ministry are we in right now?

Next Steps for Success

1. Create a list of environmental improvements that you would like to see in your area/facility. Place them in priority order and begin working to accomplish them immediately.

2. Pick up a book and a journal. Begin reading and writing intentionally.

3. When you identify the season of ministry that you are in, create a teaching lesson about it. Teach it.

SECTION III

Next Level for Success

15

Successful Relationships

Therefore encourage one another and build each
other up just as in fact you are doing.

—1 Thessalonians 5:11 (NIV)

My Greatest Regret

RECENTLY, DURING A casual conversation, one of my staff members asked me what my greatest regret or mistake in ministry was. The question caught me off guard. After all, I do not know any leader who likes to dwell on his or her mistakes. Because I have made so many goofs along the way, I would have to catalogue them and then rate them from one to ten in severity, place them in alphabetical order, and then come up with the greatest. So I asked him if I could get back to him on that one.

After thinking it through for a while, I came to this conclusion: there are many things that I could have done differently, and there are things that I did not do that I wish I had. But looking back, I believe that my biggest regret from my earlier days is that I was too selfish to see the need and benefit of investing in, training, and releasing people to do the work of ministry. What I did not know then is how much more enjoyable and fulfilling, not to mention bigger, my ministry could have been if only I had seen the need and taken the time to recruit, train, and invest in the lives of others in my ministry.

It is true, we *can* do ministry without investment in others, but ministry will be harder, less fulfilling, and contrary to Christ's example. And one day, if God decides to move us on to another location, the ministry that we spent so long building by ourselves will be greatly compromised or be nonexistent after we leave. If we think about it, investing, leading, and training the people in our ministry is an act of love and yields what is best for them and the kingdom.

Out of necessity and learning from my mistakes, I have worked to build an environment where leadership training, recruiting, and investment in the lives of people are a natural part of our ministry process. This process is not easy, and we are not perfect at it, but it has proven effective time and time again. It does not matter how big or small the church or organization, the principle is the same, and the principle was taught and demonstrated by Jesus Himself. If Jesus had not invested in the twelve disciples—teaching them, encouraging them, reprimanding them, evaluating them, and sending them out upon His departure—the work of ministry and of spreading the Gospel would have diminished significantly. It is never too early to begin a ministry of intentional investment. I used to think that I would build my own name and ministry, and then when I would be older, I would be a good mentor for someone else. The truth is, our boldest and most significant step in leadership is when we learn to recruit, lead, train, and release. We need to do it now!

If we find ourselves in a leadership rut and seem to be continually striving for the next level of ministry, it may be time to look around and begin investing in the lives of other people. If we are intentionally investing, recruiting, training, and leading, then we will be constantly growing, changing, and being challenged.

We all should look around us. Who are the potential leaders in our ministry and organization? What system or process can we put into place to develop and invest in potential leaders? Now is the time. We do not want to make the same mistake that I did in my early ministry and miss out on the fulfillment of this critical step of leadership.

Building a Relationship with the Congregation

Building a relationship with a group of people is different than building a relationship with an individual, although there are some similarities. We may not have one-on-one time with everyone in the congregation, but we do have a very important time of relationship building with them every time we meet for worship. Worship is an extremely emotional and vulnerable act, and it takes a relationship of trust and confidence for it to be effective.

First, we must be consistent. The congregation needs to know that we are going to be consistent in our leadership and in our demeanor when leading worship. There is nothing wrong with being genuinely emotional or transparent on some level some of the time. But if we are a constant emotional wreck and unstable in our walk with the Lord, we will communicate instability in our leadership from the platform. The congregation needs to know that we are on solid footing in our life and that we are in a position to lead them on a consistent basis.

Second, we must be able to communicate with them on the platform effectively. Much of this effectiveness comes from preparedness. If we are familiar with the content of our music and the order of the service, then we are more likely to be able to speak clearly and with meaning—and we can make better eye contact. If we are at ease in our role as worship leader, our congregation will be at ease as well. We need to be able to communicate genuinely and compassionately to our people.

Third, we need to love the people in our congregation enough to be willing to include songs that we do not necessarily like personally. This compromise can help lead others to a genuine worship experience. When we forget about our preference in music styles and think about leading our people to worship, the congregation will recognize the effort to bridge the musical gap, and they will be appreciative. We will never be able to make everyone happy. But we can make an effort to build a relationship with the congregation that fosters mutual respect and love for one another.

Fourth, we simply must talk to the people in our congregation and fellowship with them when we are off the platform. We would think that this is common sense, but unfortunately, it is not. We become so focused on our task ahead that we can pass by people in our hallways at church and not even notice that they are there. But guess what, they noticed that we were there and that we did not speak to them. I have found that when we take the time to walk slowly in the hallway, speak, sit, listen, love, and make an investment in the lives of the people whom we lead, they will love us for this effort. They may not always like the music selections or some of our leadership initiatives, but they will love us, and love goes a long way. Small acts of kindness and thoughtfulness add up over time and work to build a relationship with the whole congregation.

Bring a Cease-Fire to "Worship Wars"

Unfortunately, Satan has had a party with the church on the issue of worship-music decisions. We can call it the era of the worship wars. Hopefully, for most, this era is coming to an end. Let me begin by being blunt: worship wars are the result of poor leadership. The idea of arguing over music styles is futile and an ungodly behavior for people who are saved by grace and should be busy spreading the good news of the Gospel.

I grew up in a small country church with a hymnal and was not introduced to anything different until I was a teenager. We knew a lot of choruses, but we rarely sang them in worship services. Some of us are still in a similar situation—a small rural church where hymns are preferred. However, it does not matter where you are; everything continually changes. New is always coming, and we cannot escape it. Every generation creates its own voice of praise to God. I believe that there is value in all types of music—contemporary, Southern gospel, black gospel, traditional, sacred, and, yes, even bluegrass (ugh). It is our responsibility as worship leaders to teach this truth about music and then stretch our people to see the biblical perspective of how different styles of music affect our worship. No church should ever disregard new or old music. There is value in both. We cannot lose our heritage, and we cannot bury our head in the sand.

There are good hymns and bad hymns, just as there are good new worship songs and bad new worship songs. The definition of a *hymn* is this: "a song of praise to God." So by definition, all songs that are sung in praise to God are hymns. There is simply a lack of education among worship leaders and congregations. Along the years of my ministry, there have been many ways that I was able to help prevent a worship battle from breaking out. Often from the pulpit, I will call a new worship song a new hymn (which is exactly what it is). Likewise, I will call an old hymn a song of praise to God. Just this simple verbal instruction can help support the right ideas that we want our congregants to understand. We also need to educate our choir and praise team members. Music preference can easily become idolatry if we are not careful. The subject must be approached with humility and grace. Because of our selfishness, which comes from our sin, we will never fully walk away from our worship preferences because music is very emotional and powerful. Music speaks to us in ways that mere words cannot. Music is a thermostat for the soul; it turns us hot or cold. One means of success in our ministry is understanding the power and emotion that can be involved in a worship war and working to dismantle it by gently displaying the truth. Will everyone mature and grow up in this area of music preference? Unfortunately not—but we can gain ground with this issue in our churches.

Recently, I spoke with a worship leader from Mississippi. I asked him about his ministry. He explained that his church in the county seat town is the "First Baptist Church" of the town and that prejudices and tradition run deep. He told me that if he ever put a drum set on the stage, he would be out of a job. This worship pastor is also the senior adult minister. Some of the senior adults mentioned to him that it is not right to have drums and guitars in the church, and they hoped he would never bring these for worship services. In response, the worship pastor asked one of the senior adult women about the scriptures that talk about playing drums, tambourines, harps, and trumpets in worship. Her response was, "Well, I didn't think about that."

So in a nutshell, her preference and tradition of music style had turned into the sacred for her, and there was ignorance about what the Word of God says about music. I asked the worship pastor what he was doing to help educate and lead the church to mature. His response? "I don't think I can. That generation will just have to die off before we can do anything different." My heart broke, and I was stunned. It does not have to be that way! Some readers may be in a similar situation as this worship pastor. I hear the echo, "Daniel, you just don't understand." Just remember that I grew up with the *Broadman Hymnal* and shape notes for the first sixteen years of my life. I know what country, old-school, traditional worship with just a piano is like. Nevertheless, I am saying with all my heart and with all that I am that we should never be okay with the status quo. That is not a biblical or Christlike position on the matter.

I would not suggest that we incite radical changes overnight. I doubt that this approach would demonstrate love for our people very well. In fact, I'm sure that if the worship leader from the Mississippi county seat First Baptist Church were to place the drum set on the platform the next week without any relational preparation, he would probably need to update his résumé by Monday morning. However, we can regularly and systematically disciple our congregations on the biblical truths of worship. But guess what—this process is hard ministry work, and it takes patience, love, humility, and a little bit of tough skin. Guess what happens when the Word of God is taught? Truth is revealed, and God draws a line in the sand. There have been a few ways that I have had some systematic and intentional times of discipleship on biblical worship.

First, I teach my choir and orchestra about biblical worship. I have multiple generations represented by age in our music ministry program, which helps with worship discipleship. Second, I have made myself available at the senior adult monthly luncheons when possible. In the early years at Westside, I would ask to be on the speaking docket at least twice a year. I used this time to sing with them then share my heart and teach about church music history, biblical worship, etc. Third, occasionally, I teach a Bible study on biblical worship open to participation by anyone in the church family. Fourth, I am always looking for opportunities to use phrases, words, and ideas in our worship times together to support the practice of biblical worship. I cannot believe how many times God has used some of these avenues to create breakthroughs in our mutigenerational worship.

Some senior adults who once stood with arms folded when we sang anything different than a familiar hymn now stand and sing with joy. And youth and college students who would roll their eyes at an old hymn now lift their hands in praise to "Great Is Thy Faithfulness." We see a beautiful thing when God uses His Word to transform the lives of the people whom we serve. We need to make clear the point—it is not our job to change our people, and if we make the effort alone, we will only get frustrated and either resign or be fired. It is God's work through the Holy Spirit and His Word to change the hearts of His people. It is, however, our job to teach them the Word and disciple and equip them to be worshipers of God.

One final word: if someone is struggling with these issues, surrender this war, but do not give up.

Dealing with Conflict

No matter how wonderful our church may be, at some point, we will deal with conflict. Why? Because we are people, and we will never always agree. If we agreed with one another on everything all the time, then life would be perfect! Or would it?

Actually, the Lord gave us minds and personal experiences so that we could look at things differently and, therefore, each make a contribution to the whole in a unique way. Usually we view conflict as negative, and in instances when the people involved become offensive or demeaning, it can possibly be a negative thing. But I am going to suggest that conflict can often be a positive event and a learning opportunity. Over the years, I have certainly learned a lot about myself when dealing with conflict. I have learned to try to prevent conflict as much as possible by communicating well and doing good thinking. But even with our best intentions and extensive planning, there will be times when we will be in conflict with someone or a group of people.

Back in 2003, my wife and I were visiting a megachurch and were able to spend some time with the minister of music. Thinking that people in large churches had it made and did not have to deal with the same petty issues that I did in a smaller church, I asked him, "Do you ever have people who disagree with what you do or complain about this or that?" His answer was stunning to me, and I have never forgotten what he told me. He said, "Of course! But instead of individuals, they just come in groups now." I asked him what he would say to people who opposed something regarding his leadership. He said, "I listen to them and then ask them to pray for us as we seek to do the best we can for all involved." His answer has followed me to this very day. This simple statement has made a profound impact on how I deal with conflict. Here are some principles to draw from when we have to manage conflict:

1. *Seek to understand.* Listen carefully to what the other person or persons are trying to communicate to you. Ask more questions than make statements. Sometimes we find that petty complaints are often not the root of the real issue. Pettiness is a symptom of a greater issue. So someone may come in complaining about blinding lighting, and then with some good questions, we realize that he or she is hurting and feeling discounted about something that is completely unrelated to the initial complaint. When this is the case, we have a chance to love and minister.

2. *Never be rude.* Always keep in mind that just because people disagree with us does not mean that they deserve to be treated with disrespect. It simply means that they do not see things the way we do. Respect them enough to disagree with kindness.

3. *Work for a win-win scenario.* There is rarely a reason why someone has to lose or be discounted because of differences of opinion. Often, good communication will go a long way when resolving conflict.

4. *Do not be passive-aggressive.* Passive-aggressive behavior is destructive and is not beneficial to anyone. A passive-aggressive person may appear to agree—perhaps even enthusiastically—with another person's request, but

actually will disagree with that person by doing the opposite of what was agreed to do or by avoiding or ignoring the request altogether.

5. *Speak with humility, but with a gentle strength.* Humility absolutely does not mean being weak and timid. Humility, in this context, is understanding that we do not know everything and that the world does not revolve around us and our line of thinking. There will be times when we will need to lead through a conflict with humility and gentle strength. I equate gentle strength to standing my ground without dismissing the fruits of the Spirit and negotiating under the leadership of the Holy Spirit.

I wish that I could say that these principles are always easy to adhere to. In fact, they can certainly be challenging to remember and apply. But I promise that most conflicts can be diffused by a lot of love, good communication, and respect and appreciation for one another. However, there are those occasions when someone will approach us with the wrong spirit and not be willing to seek a resolution. Instead, they want to tear us down and posture to prove a point. In these cases, we must still work to apply all these principles but understand that we may have to walk away and that we will never see eye to eye with this person. When we find this to be the case, we can love and pray for this person, stand our ground with gentle strength, but then end the conversation and move on.

Successful Relationship between the Worship Pastor and the Senior Pastor

In any successful worship ministry, there must be a strong relationship between the worship pastor and the senior pastor. This relationship is special and is different than any other staff relationship. The senior pastor and the worship pastor are the most visible staff members in the church because of their platform positions. This reality should not downplay any other staff position, and it does not suggest that the worship pastor holds a position of greater importance. However, the worship pastor and the senior pastor need a chemistry that is seen and heard by the members of the congregation. The worship pastor is of service to the senior pastor's leadership, and their public work together should be a marriage of ministry dynamics.

While writing this section, I sat down with my pastor, and we discussed our relationship. We laughed about the early days of learning about each other and reminisced fondly on the incredible Spirit-filled moments that we have shared together. I asked him to help me with this section by answering a few questions that readers might want to have answered:

What does a senior pastor want most from his worship pastor?
Senior pastors want a worship pastor who has a passionate pursuit of God in life and ministry. Singers and musicians are a dime a dozen. Talent alone is not enough to make someone a good worship leader. But a pastor wants to lead with someone who is in pursuit of God in all areas of life and is obeying a call in worship ministry leadership.

Second, a senior pastor wants to have an authentic relationship with his worship pastor. While there is a healthy barrier that must be maintained between a pastor and a staff member, there is a vulnerability that has to be present with a pastor and a worship pastor. This vulnerability does not mean that there is an absence of boundaries, but it does mean that there is an understanding about a little more transparency in the relationship.

Third, trust between the senior pastor and the worship pastor is critical. There is a high level of confidentiality that must be present for a strong bond to exist. Public platform chemistry will be absent if there is not a private trust and love between the senior pastor and the worship pastor. By the way, there is no way that a lack of trust can be hidden from the congregation; no one will be fooled.

As a high-capacity/output leader, how do pastors generally want information relayed to them?

The answer to this question is very dependent on the personality of the leader. I have always liked information in writing, but very brief and concise writing. Most pastors like to see a plan on paper. They want to know that an idea has been well-thought-out and has made it out of the recesses of our brains or off the napkin and onto a piece of paper. Often, worship pastors are creative people who can dream and not be very organized with their thoughts or information. They have to learn to communicate their ideas to our pastor in a professional and concise way.

Finally, a high-capacity/output pastor would rather talk with a staff person face-to-face rather than through e-mail. E-mails should be saved for sharing or confirming information. They should not be used for confrontation or conversation. There is no way to communicate emotion, passion, feelings, and intentions through an e-mail or text message. Relational maters should be communicated face-to-face.

What are the few things that build trust the fastest with staff/ worship pastors?

First would be an evidence of spiritual vitality in their lives. People are much more understanding and forgiving if they know or sense that there is progress and maturity happening in the staff member's life. Second, it is extremely important that commitments made are kept. It is never a good idea to be flippant about not keeping a commitment. Trust is built only when we do what we say, when we say, how we say. When we fail to do that, then trust will diminish quickly. Last, there is no room for silos on a team. A pastor wants to see that his worship pastor is demonstrating interest in the welfare of the staff as a whole. A worship pastor can sometimes be the eyes and ears for the senior pastor within a staff. For this to be most effective, the worship pastor needs to look beyond his or her own wishes and desires and be able to view things from a team perspective.

What do you wish you had more of when it comes to your relationship with your worship pastor?

I wish I could have more time. Ministry is demanding, and often senior pastors and worship pastors cannot have a lot of time together. But the time we do have needs to be of quality and productive.

One of the keys to having a successful relationship with my pastor is knowing what he wants, when he wants it, how he wants it. It was a joy to be able to learn his expectations and then figure out how to exceed them. Because I know that my pastor likes things in writing, I do not recall a time that I have ever gone into my pastor's office for a meeting without something in writing to show him. He appreciates that simple gesture of respect that I offer to our relationship.

From the beginning, I decided that I wanted our pastor to be included in the new music that I was listening to. He purchased an iPod, and I loaded it with all the latest things that I was listening to. If I buy a song, I make sure he has access to it. When we meet, we are constantly asking, "Have you heard this song?" and we will share. It is these simple things that go above and beyond that can make a difference.

Let me stop right here before anyone gets the wrong idea. I am not, nor have I never been, a yes-man when it comes to my relationship with my pastor. There were those few moments where we had to speak the kind of truths that sting. It is rare, but it happens in any real and loving relationship. To be anything but honest and true to my heart with my senior pastor is to not love well. My interest is not in my pastor liking me because I agree with everything that he says. My interest is what is best for the people whom we serve and the kingdom of Christ and how I can support and serve my pastor in leading them to be all they can be.

If we go in with that attitude, then when it is time to agree, we agree and move on. When it is time to disagree, we disagree, discuss, come to an agreement or agree to disagree, and move on. It is that simple. We have had staff members come and go over the years, and some of them did not learn this principle of relating to their senior pastor and aligning with his vision for the church. Alignment and unity of vision empower staff persons and give them a freedom. My pastor has always sought to empower my ministry. He often gives verbal praise from the pulpit, for which I am grateful. He sends texts and e-mails reflecting his love and support. Almost without fail, he asks me how he can help me. Not only has this affirmation strengthened me as a staff person and given me confidence in my ministry, it has given me a snapshot into his heart and his care for me and for our staff and our church.

Can I speak truth here? If any worship pastor cannot get behind the vision and direction of their senior pastors, then they need to bow out gracefully and go serve somewhere else. A worship pastor and a senior pastor who are at odds is no secret to anyone, and it is seen visibly on the platform whether we say anything to anyone or not. If we are committed to our calling from God and love the people whom we serve, then we do the church and ourselves a favor and move on.

Relationships with People in the Community

Our connection to the community is a huge, super, gigantic step in moving our ministry from survival to success. I only regret that I did not learn this sooner and build it as a discipline in my ministry.

I do not know anyone who does community contacts better than my dad, Harold. He is a pastor in North Florida. He knows the art of being in the community. Everyone in the city seems to know who my dad is. He builds time each week in his schedule to visit not only the hospitals and nursing homes but also his church members' businesses. He will stop by to see them, meet others, and invite them to church. Because he is well-known in the community, he pastors a very vibrant growing congregation.

I am not a naturally outgoing person, so this had to be a learned skill and a discipline for me, which has come out of being in an environment where having strategic community contacts is taught and expected. To be honest, I still struggle with this discipline. It is a constant chore for me to seek community people in whom I should invest. But as I have prayed about who God would have me engage in the community, he always brings someone to mind or in my path. It is very easy to allow the organization and tasks of ministry to bog us down and never allow us to leave our desk. That is why we have to be intentional about putting this activity on our schedule.

We live in a city with a major university and a large state college. So naturally, some of my intentional connections are with the music and media departments within these schools. We have worked to set up partnerships and develop ministries that would benefit the student as well as our church. Through internships, workshops, and seminars on our campus, we have been able to make a connection. I have also worked to be on discussion panels and serve as guest instructor or representative in the classrooms as much as possible. Breakfasts and lunches on certain days are reserved for meetings with strategic businesspersons in our community. In our staff/team environment, we are often encouraged to make arrangements with local businesses to just stop by and pray for and with the employees before they begin their day. These simple community connections are critical for long-term growth and ministry success. These relationships are things that go beyond the music ministry to show that we love and care about not only the people whom we serve in our church but also the people whom they work with who are not yet part of our church. It makes a statement about us and a statement about our churches, and it is a good one!

We may have the opportunity to start a Bible study with some community business owners. Just recently, the Lord put on my heart to pray for the businesses that I pass on my way to the office. When I got to my desk, I contacted many of them by e-mail just to say that I prayed for them and their businesses that morning. The response was incredible! They were so appreciative. Whatever opportunities the Lord gives us, we need to be faithful to build relationships within our communities. It will be a catalyst to help move ministry from survival to success.

Questions for Reflection

1. Are you more task driven or relationship driven?
2. What adjustments do you need to make to have a balance of tasks and building strong relationships?
3. Do you have a healthy relationship with your congregation? Do they trust and respect your leadership?
4. Are you offering consistent, strong, caring, and theologically sound leadership each week?
5. How are you seeking to grow a relationship with your senior pastor?

Next Steps for Success

1. Take time to think and pray through a list of about ten to twelve people within your ministry whom you can build a

relationship with. Could any of these people help you in your ministry? Why not ask if you can train them?

2. Seek to build a relationship with your congregation by lovingly addressing any worship differences. Be proactive instead of reactive.

3. Initiate time with your pastor. Sit down with him and ask if there is anything that you can do to help his ministry. Take good notes and try hard to meet his needs within your ability to do so.

4. Identify some key businesses in your immediate perimeter. Gather the proper information about their businesses and begin to pray for them systematically. Let them know that you are praying and ask them if they have any specific prayer requests. Let them know that you care.

16

Marriage Between Music and Media

> And above all these put on love, which binds
> everything together in perfect harmony.
>
> —Colossians 3:14 (NIV)

FOR SIXTEEN YEARS, my family traveled and sang gospel music in the southeastern United States. We had our own sound system that we had to set up in a different venue every time we performed. During those years, I learned about improvisation with sound systems. We just had to make it work no matter what! Because of these experiences, I assumed that music ministers should work very closely with the sound and tech crews. To my surprise, this is not always reality. In fact, many worship leaders stay at odds with their media and technical teams. Often the reason is that we do not all speak the same language, and there is a huge communication barrier between these two important ministries. Because of this barrier, there seems be a distinct lack of appreciation for each other.

I decided from the beginning of my ministry that I would always try to stay close to my media personnel. Danny was my first volunteer soundman when I went on staff at a church while I was in seminary. Danny and I quickly became the best of friends. I initiated getting to know him and worked to develop an understanding of his perspective on his ministry. As it turned out, he worked his hardest to make sure that we were successful on the platform each week. He always went above and beyond when it came to our shared ministry.

When I came to my current place of service, I knew that the expansive ministry that we had made it important for our departments to be closely connected. After a short transition period, I was able to organize our ministry title from the music and worship ministry to the music, worship, and media ministry. It was an organizational change that reflected my values and priorities. When I had the chance to hire my first full-time media person, I found someone who understood both music and media extensively. I hired him as my associate minister of music and media. He was second-in-command under me on the music and worship side, and he was the executive minister over our entire media ministry. This proved to be one of the best decisions that I have ever made.

Today our Music and Media ministries are tightly connected and interlinked. Every music decision is made with a media perspective and vice versa. As a result, the nearly twenty volunteers in our media ministry know nothing different from the idea of music and media ministries working together. All of them are well equipped to serve our music and worship ministry very well. Our current configuration no longer calls for a minister of music and media. But even with just a full-time minister of media, the culture has already been established and our continual, consistent approach to ministry life is still the same. Our media personnel all attend our departmental staff meetings, and our minister of media always attends our worship-planning meetings.

If a worship pastor frequently gets frustrated at the media and sound crew, there is hope.

The first thing to do is to work at becoming close with those who serve us each week. We do not have to be best friends with them, but we should take the time to learn about these persons and understand how they think, respond, and operate. We should also take the time to know and learn about their families, dreams, interests, and hobbies. Second, we should learn to speak their language. Ask them for training in what they do every week so that you can understand their perspective. It can be extremely frustrating to our sound crew if we do not know what certain pieces of equipment are called or how things are meant to work. This lack of knowledge throws up a huge communication barrier. Finally, we need to meet with our media person or team as often as we can, once a week if possible. This effort will yield the greatest results with the least frustrations and produce our best each week. In the end, it is a matter of respect and love. We must seek to understand how the media minister or sound person is trying to support us. We need to work to have a good relationship with those who make us sound and look good.

Fortunately, I have been blessed with some good sound and media personnel in my ministry. I have also had the experience of not having the best support from the sound booth. Early in my ministry, I had a technical and media director who did not possess the capacity to grow and provide the proper support for our shared ministries. He always tried to explain to me the reasons why he would not be able to do what I asked him to do. In the end, I knew that if I allowed it, this one individual would single-handedly hold back our ministry. I knew that I had to act decisively. After months of administrative processes to place us in a positive position to move forward together, I came to understand that this working relationship would not be a win-win. So I developed an exhaustive set of expectations, in writing, that would need to be followed with no exceptions. After reviewing the expectations, this person decided that he would not be able to meet the required expectations and behaviors necessary for moving forward. Therefore, we had to end our shared ministry together. This person was able to dismiss himself with dignity and grace to follow the Lord and His calling elsewhere.

On paper, this may seem like a very simple and easy series of events, but it was not. It was one of the more difficult moments in my ministry. Ministry and relationships with people can get complicated and messy. But there is one thing that we have to keep in mind: we must love well. Loving well does not always mean that things will be happy and easy and people will get what they want. In fact, love demands some of the most difficult decisions and tasks from us. For me to love our ministry participants well, I needed to put us in the best possible position to move forward. And for me to love this particular staff person well, I did not need to keep him in a position that would hold back ministry and breed continual frustrations. Some of us may be in situations where we need to work on our relationships and get them moving in the right direction so that we can move ministry forward and create a win-win scenario for everyone involved. Some of us may owe our sound and media crew a heartfelt apology for not understanding how to communicate and work together for the overall health and growth of the church. Then there are some of us who may need finally to love enough to confront some issues and personalities that need to change or be dismissed. Whatever our situation, we must bathe every action in prayer and ask that the Holy Spirit guide us in this area of ministry discipleship.

Finally, our goal must be to bond the ministries of music and media together organizationally, relationally, and spiritually. We should be praying together, dreaming together, and working hard together. We can share one another's ministry burdens, look out for one another, and love one another. This simple process has the potential to enhance us in our Sunday morning ministry and create many years of successful kingdom impact.

Questions for Reflection

1. How is the relationship between your worship ministry and your media ministry?
2. What can you do this week to strengthen your ministry relationship with your media or sound person/team?

Next Steps for Success

1. Schedule some time with your media/sound person to just hang out and talk.
2. Schedule a regular meeting with your media/sound person so that you can plan and discuss upcoming services.
3. Create a list of media expectations that you have for a worship service or a rehearsal. Spend some intentional time discussing the expectations with your media/sound person. Agree on actions, language, responses, and behaviors that reflect your ministry's priorities and desired results.

17

Our Ministry and Our World Becoming a Great Commission Leader

And Jesus came and said to them, "All authority in heaven and on earth has been given to me. Go therefore and make disciples of all nations, baptizing them in the name of the Father and of the Son and of the Holy Spirit, teaching them to observe all that I have commanded you. And behold, I am with you always, to the end of the age."

—Matthew 28:18–20 (NIV)

Being a Great Commission Leader

THE GREAT COMMISSION is pretty clear. We are to go and make disciples. This statement is intended for the entire body of Christ. We often think of missions in terms of missionaries sent overseas. But the Great Commission and the act of going and making disciples are for every believer. If believers are actively carrying out the Great Commission, then they will automatically be missional. Further, someone in an authentic worship relationship with

Christ will have an urgency for obeying the Great Commission. Worship and missions go hand in hand. In fact, missions is an act of worship because to be missional is to be obedient to the call of Christ, which applies to every follower.

Unfortunately, this criterion for a true worshipper of Christ narrows the field down. Am I saying that all believers have to have a passport to be legitimate in their faith? No. But what I am saying is that true worship connects us to the heart of God. And what pleases the heart of God is that all would know Him and be in obedient relationship with Him. Therefore, we should not only be diligently obeying the Great Commission locally, but we also should be ready to go abroad in whatever capacity that the Lord should call us. Do I have a passport? Absolutely.

Being a Worshipper on Mission

The work of missions is the work of every believer, even worship pastors. Our church is serious about our global missions commitment. It is expected that every member of our ministerial staff attend or lead a national or international mission trip every year. I am very grateful that my environment has given me this gift. Active missions have shaped a culture within our church that is unique and has brought about a unity and a sweet spirit within our people. There is something about having a global perspective of ministry that makes us see what we do on our own church campus differently. I promise that once we experience worship on mission, our leadership and attitude will be changed for the good.

I understand that not all churches have the same mission emphasis that we do, so that is why I am writing this section. We can be a leader for our churches in this area. Although a church with a heart for missions ultimately has to be cultivated by the senior pastor, we can have influence in this area and have a great platform from which to do it—music.

I implore every music minister to figure out a way to go on a mission trip, especially an international mission trip. There are many opportunities to join short-term mission trips through larger churches, associations, state and national conventions, etc. This experience on the field will change lives and ministry perspectives.

Next time, we will want to take someone with us! It does not matter if we take one person or two hundred people with us, this mission experience is the next step of discipleship and development for our people. As a worship pastor, if we want to move from a place of survival to a ministry of success, and if we want to build an attitude and spirit of unity among our people, we should get as many people as we can on mission. They will come back changed, and our ministry will begin to look and feel different. I believe that one of the reasons that our people have such a kingdom mind-set and a worship mentality is that many of them have been on a mission trip.

First, we can explore the possibilities. We can begin now to pray about where God would have us go. We can make missions a priority by building mission trips in our yearly budget. We could take our youth choir, adult choir, or praise team on a mission trip. We can plan to sing or play an instrument, but we don't have to! It can be any type of mission work in which a person uses whatever he or she is passionate about or good at. Because of the incredible task before us to reach the world, the work should always be strategic and include opportunities to share the Gospel and disciple believers.

Once we have experienced the powerful and life-changing event known as the mission trip, then we will want to turn our focus on training others to lead teams. Multiplying our leadership is critical to keep this missional spirit alive within our churches and ministries. We have teams from our choir and orchestra leaving all the time. We often commission them during a choir rehearsal. Over the past year, I have been encouraging my care group leaders to lead their care group to go on a mission trip. It would be so great if we had several groups of our choir and orchestra joining in strategic work all over the world, sharing the Gospel and coming back changed by the work of the Holy Spirit in their lives. I'm telling you, this is a major step toward moving our ministries forward and making an impact for the cause of Christ outside of our normal Sunday morning worship services. Worship missions will bring a whole new depth to us as leaders and to our ministries.

Because of the relationships that we have built, we now have invitations often asking us to go places around the world teaching about music, leadership, and evangelism.

Being a Missional Worshipper

We certainly understand that missions involve more than participating in a mission trip or a mission service project. In fact, missions go beyond the temporary and become a lifestyle. I refer to this step as being a missional worshipper or being a Great Commission worshipper. "If the heartbeat of worship is obedience, then it is impossible to be a true worshipper without being directly involved in the command of evangelism as expressed in Acts 1:8."[1]

Missions and worship go hand in hand. They cannot be separated. We often think of worship as something that we do when we gather together in community and praise the Lord together. Corporate worship is just one of many expressions of the worship of God. The eternal purpose of our lives should be to bring glory to God in every way! To allow our lives to be controlled by the Holy Spirit and to move in obedience to His

---

1   David Wheeler and Vernon M. Whaley, *The Great Commission to Worship: Biblical Principles for Worship-Based Evangelism*, Original ed. (Nashville: B&H Academic, 2011), 13.

Word and promptings is to live a lifestyle of worship. Being a missional worshipper is living out our worship every day. If we are worshipping in Spirit and in truth, then our hearts will be transformed to be more like Christ. Our thoughts and actions will be captive to the things of Christ. At the heart of missional worship is Jesus. In their book, *The Great Commission to Worship*, David Wheeler and Vernon M. Whaley describe a life of a missional worshipper:

> There are many people around us who are busy about evangelism and yet never bow their knee or lift their hands in worship. They are busy doing ministry. There are some who sing songs and lift their hands and yet never share the gospel with their neighbors. They are in love with worship. A worshipping saint (one who has completely fallen in love with Jesus), one who loves Jesus for all that He is and all that He does (one who thoroughly understands the transformational power of worship), will always engage in evangelism. It is totally impossible for the person who truly worships in spirit and truth not to demonstrate the wonder of God in their life.[2]

This kind of lifestyle requires sacrifice. It also requires us to be held accountable to the command of the Word of God. I must admit that when I first began to think of being a missional worshipper, I realized that I was not fully engaged in that way. I would have probably fallen into the category of either being completely involved in ministry matters or being in love with worshipping—but not fully invested in the idea of being a missional worshipper. This commitment is something that I have to ask God continually to help me do. The truth is, we cannot be this kind of worshipper in our own strength. We do not have

2   Ibid., 51-52.

the capacity to live a life in this way; it must be the work of the Holy Spirit in our lives. "The Holy Spirit equips, fills, energizes, and empowers worshippers to declare the wonders of God to the lost."[3]

Questions for Reflection

1. Am I a missional worshipper, or am I just in love with worship or ministry?
2. What can I do to develop a mission priority in my ministry?
3. Is there a mission opportunity that I could be involved in locally or internationally?

Next Steps for Success

1. Get your passport.
2. Begin to pray about and seek a mission opportunity. Check with your local association or convention to see if there are opportunities that you can connect with.
3. Ask or challenge someone in your ministry to do a mission trip with you.
4. Pray that God would give you a heart for worship that is missional and seeks to glorify Christ in all ways.

---

3   Ibid., 51.

18

Learning How to Be Successful with Others

> God's definition of success is really one of *significance*—the significant difference our lives can make in the lives of others.
>
> —Tony Dungy

LIFE IS NOT successfully lived alone. We see the heart of God on this matter in Genesis when He made Eve to be a helpmate for Adam. I was far too old before I realized the reality of this truth and did anything about it. We need people in our lives with whom we can do life and ministry.

Having a Mentor

We can learn a lot from someone else. We can learn what to do, but we can also learn what not to do. The challenge is always to be in a mode of learning. Some of the greatest lessons learned in ministry were the result of observing the mistakes of others and how those mistakes affected ministry. Many of us, however, are prone to take the hard road of trying to figure out everything for ourselves. What no one tells us is that solo learning is harder and slower. Learning comes so much faster if we can watch and apply life and ministry lessons from someone else.

Everyone needs a mentor. What is a mentor? A mentor is someone who can give intentional investment of his or her time to help in a life or ministry process. I was not fortunate enough to realize my need of mentors early in my ministry; however, I was blessed to have them appear in my life. My mentors came out of position and circumstance. Two of them happened to be the pastors of the churches where I was serving. One of my current mentors, Tony, was a guest with our staff doing a leadership seminar. I immediately felt that I needed to connect with him and learn as much as I possibly could. I was nervous to ask him but came to the point where I was not going to let the fear of rejection stop me from connecting with someone I felt could help me accomplish the vision that God had placed in my heart. So I asked him, and he graciously accepted. Tony helped me identify and organize my life goals and dreams. He began challenging me on accomplishing those dreams, including the writing of this book.

I have asked others if they would mentor me only to have been told no or "not at this time." If that happens, it is all right. We have to trust that the Lord has someone else whom He is preparing to help us accomplish our calling. Just know we do not have to do ministry alone. There are those heavyweights in the faith and in the ministry who are ready and eager to help us. All we have to do is identify those persons and ask. My three or four mentors whom I have in my life are all very active in communicating with me and in speaking into my life. They each serve a different purpose and encourage me in different ways. Having a mentor speaks volumes about how we view ourselves. It says that we are still learning and that we value those whom God has placed in our path to learn from.

When we have identified and secured a mentor, we must never let a moment go by unprepared to learn from that individual. We will want to take full advantage of someone who is investing his or her time and energy in us. Even after several years with the same mentors, I still answer the phone with a notepad and pen ready to write down any and everything I can.

Being a Mentor

Many make the mistake of seeing mentoring as a very time-consuming activity and may shy away from making this important step in their ministry. As we grow in our influence and leadership, mentoring will likely become a natural step in the process. It is not necessary to think of mentoring as "pouring" our life into someone else, but a better way to think of this is "investing" in someone else. Pouring gives a picture of someone opening up their whole life and drenching the other person with everything they know, leaving the mentor empty with nothing left to give (which is why we sometimes shy away from this idea). Investing in someone gives the idea that there is a decided amount of time and energy invested with a potential beneficial return—a win-win perspective.

When choosing whom to invest in, we need to think carefully. Sometimes this choice will be easy and obvious, but often, opportunities to invest can come as a surprise or even an intentional move on our part to look for someone to mentor. For those times when it is not an easy, obvious choice, here are some thoughts when deciding to become a mentor.

First, we want to choose to invest in someone who has a teachable spirit and wants to learn from us. It is very tiring and discouraging to invest time in someone who could care less about what you have to say. There are some people who do not have the capacity to learn from others. They have to learn for themselves. We should refrain from investing too much time in these people.

Second, we should invest in someone who has vision and realistic goals for his or her future. It is hard to help someone nail Jell-O to a wall. What I mean by that is, as a mentor, we want to help people achieve their goals and be all that they can be, but the person we are investing in must have a good sense of self-awareness. While I believe we can do anything we set our minds to, within reason, there are just some endeavors that are unrealistic for some people. We have to use discretion and common sense when seeking whom to mentor.

Third, we want to invest in people who are self-motivated and eager to do something with their life. Nothing can be more exhaustive than having continually to push someone just to keep up with the basics. The person whom we choose to mentor needs to be someone who will take our investment in them and quickly turn around and begin to invest in others. At this point, they are multiplying our investment. This "reinvestment" is a great indication that we are doing the right thing with the right person. If we choose to mentor someone who does not have the capacity to invest in others, then our efforts will soon be used up with no sustaining outcome.

Mentoring can take on different forms. It does not have to be extensive and consume a huge amount of our time. I live in Florida, and one of my mentors lives in Dallas, Texas, and the other in Enterprise, Alabama. So there are no weekly meetings. The extent of our communication is through texts, e-mails, and phone calls. I am challenged and encouraged by these persons, who make me think with a well-formed question or a simple quotation. They may ask me to read something to discuss it the next time we talk by phone. They make recommendations. They guide, pray for, and share insights with me. In fact, both of my mentors are helping me with the process of this book. I started writing because of the encouragement of my mentor to begin something that has been on my life-goals list for years.

When we become a mentor, we have the chance to influence in ways that we could never do otherwise. We can invest our insights, experiences, and encouragement into someone else. The hope is that we will equip someone that we mentor to become a mentor to someone else.

Just recently, I have started mentoring our family financial advisor. He is a successful insurance-and-investment agent whom I have grown to trust and appreciate. While meeting about our finances, our friendship developed, and we began to swap stories. He began sharing with me one day about how he would like to move to the next level in leadership within his company. I was sharing with him insights about some simple ways that he could increase his influence within his organization. I suggested a book that I thought would help him. I offered to read it with him if he wanted to stop by my office once a week for three weeks to discuss how we could apply what we were reading. He agreed. Thus began our mentoring relationship. As we began to meet, we developed a great friendship. Not only did he move up in his company and become one of the company's best agents, he eventually left the agency to start his own business career. Now he is actively meeting and investing in others just as I invested in him.

It is a given that I always spend one-on-one mentoring time with my staff. Sharing and developing with them brings us closer together and allows us to do better work. We have another staff person in a different department who is meeting with twelve high school students each week and reading a leadership book with them. It is incredible, the stories that have come from that group of students. They are growing and learning to invest in others, and the group has grown as they have gained influence with their friends.

One final thought: while every relationship should be a win-win situation, we must never choose to mentor or enter into relationship for selfish reasons or for personal advancement. These are ungodly and unethical motivations. In the end, these kinds of relationships will never work, and both you and your mentee will lose.

Questions for Reflection

1. Are you lonely in ministry? If so, why?
2. Are you currently being officially mentored by someone?
3. Are you intentionally investing in the life of someone else on a consistent basis?

Next Steps for Success

1. Make a list of the people whom you can involve in your personal ministry. Begin to
2. Take someone with you when you make a ministry visit or are doing a ministry task.
3. Identify a potential mentor and a mentee and then ask them to join you on your ministry journey.

19

Networking for Success

The opposite of networking is not working.

—Someone smart

NETWORKING IS A very strategic and intentional step when seeking to move from survival to success. We will want to network with as many people as possible who are not on our church campuses. Finding those around us whom we can learn from and talk to about ministry and certain aspects of our job can be very beneficial. Networking can happen anywhere. One place where we can start is through our association or community of churches. Perhaps there are some events where we can connect with other worship pastors whom we can learn from or even help out. Another great place to network is conferences. One of the things I like most about a worship conference is the opportunity to connect with other worship pastors and staff members. It might even be a bad conference where we are not getting much out of the presented materials or sessions, but if there are people around us, there is an opportunity to network. We have to be prepared to network by having a business card or something that can be easily exchanged when meeting someone. We may even exchange contacts through our smartphones. Whatever our method, it is helpful to be able to connect with others who do what we do.

One important aspect of networking is the kind of people that we network with. It is not very beneficial and fairly unpractical to network with everyone we meet. Here are some guidelines that our former senior pastor Dr. Gary Crawford taught us to use when seeking to network with someone:

- *Network with someone who is behind us.* This person could be in a ministry situation that is slightly smaller in size than ours, or this might be someone younger and just starting out in his or her ministry. Perhaps there may be a way to connect with this ministry to aid and challenge them in some way.
- *Network with someone who is with us.* This person would have a similar-size worship program or have some of the same ministry struggles and strengths as we do. It is always fun to share ideas that can be applied immediately back and forth.
- *Network with someone who is ahead of us.* There is always someone who is one step ahead of where we are. It may be challenging, but we can make the decision to network with someone from whom we can learn and who may be a silent or maybe even an intentional mentor for us and our ministry in the future.
- *Network with someone who intimidates us.* Persons at the top of the field may seem "unreachable" to connect with, but we may be surprised at how willing and eager they might be to network with us and give us the chance to learn from what they do.

Back in 2003, I was sitting at my desk in our church in Alabama listening to music from a music preview pack that had come in the mail. I pulled out the book of youth choir music and popped in the CD to give it a listen. I loved it. I loved everything about it. The music was fresh; the pictures of the choir on the cover of the book were lively and interesting. I remember flipping to the back cover of the book to see what church had recorded the CD. It was a large church in Texas.

At that point, I had only served in smaller churches; I was unfamiliar and unexposed to a large-church ministry environment. However, I was so impressed that I wanted to know more about this ministry, so I began to do some research. The more I found out about the ministry that was happening at this church, the more I wanted to learn. So nervously I called and inquired about coming for a visit. Enthusiastically and to my surprise, the music staff welcomed the opportunity for me and my wife to come and spend a few days with them. I was stunned! I had not expected that they would actually be willing for me to come and "bother" them for a few days. At the time, I did not realize how much this trip to network with a church and people that intimidated me would completely change my ministry.

When we arrived, we walked into this beautiful massive building. My wife was well poised and seemed very calm and collected. I, on the other hand, had to hold my hand under my bottom jaw to keep it from dragging the floor. My eyes were wide, and I temporarily lost the ability to blink. I did not want to miss anything. The details of the parking lot, the water fountain, the foyer were exquisite and certainly bigger than anything this young country boy had ever seen! We walked up to the guest-services counter and told them who we were. They said, "Hello, Mr. and Mrs. Morris, we are expecting you. I'll call the music department and tell them that you are here." We did not wait long before the music receptionist rounded the corner. She met us with warmth and took us on a brief tour.

As we were walking down the hallway, we would pass people who would look at me and say, "Hey, Mr. Morris." I leaned over to my wife and asked, "How do they know who we are?" Terri, the receptionist, overheard me and said, "We have prepared for your arrival, and everyone around here knows who you are." I was floored. As we were introduced to each music staff person—at the time, all thirteen of them—my wife and I were both greeted by our first names in every case without fail. Eventually, I realized how and why they were able to do that. At some point, the staff did some research on who we were, where we were from, and several points of interest about us. They created a bio sheet with our pictures and gave them to all the relative staff members who might have contact with us the week we were there. That was how people passing in the hallways knew who we were and could call us by name. This preparation was such wonderful detail that I had never realized could make such a huge impression on my experience.

While meeting with the staff, I asked a ton of questions about how they do what they do. We were invited to special dinners and lunches, meetings, rehearsals. They were so kind to us. But most of all, I learned what they do by observing every room setup, every process, every systematic approach—from their office- and ministry-area layout to the computer software that they used to do certain functions. I watched closely at the choir rehearsal how they managed so many people, about five hundred, in the choir. I watched how they passed out music, how their leadership communicated with them, and how they taught them style, diction, and musicality in a fun and worshipful environment. I took note of every detail. It is probably safe to say that I learned more in those few days about practical music ministry than I did in any classroom or from any book. Seeing a high-expectation and intricately detailed ministry in action was pivotal for my future.

Twelve years later, I still have a ministry that reflects principles and details that I learned on that trip to Texas. I am grateful for their willingness to take the time to invest in us that week. I doubt they could ever know what their small investment did to an impressionable, teachable young worship pastor like me. I will always be grateful for those few days there and am glad that I took the chance to network with an organization that intimidated me.

Questions for Reflection

1. What opportunities are around you for networking?
2. Who is currently in your network?
3. Who is the Lord bringing to your mind whom you should try to connect with?

Next Steps for Success

1. Make a list of people or places that you need to go to network.
2. Make yourself available for others to network with you.
3. Pray that God would guide you to grow in the area of networking and connecting with others.

20

Taking the Next Steps Toward Success

"The price of success is hard work, dedication to the job at hand, and the determination that whether we win or lose, we have applied the best of ourselves to the task at hand."

—Vince Lombardi[1]

IN HIS BOOK *Developing the Leader Within You*, John Maxwell teaches about five basic levels of leaders. There are the "position leaders," leaders based solely on their position within the organization. People have to follow them whether they want to or not. Next is the "permission leader." This is leadership based on relationships. People follow this person because they want to. Third is the "production leader." This leader is working at a level to produce bottom-line results within the organization. People follow this leader because of what he or she has done for the organization. Fourth, there is the "people development leader." People will follow these leaders because of what they have done

---

1   Vince Lombardi, *Run to Daylight! Vince Lombardi's Diary of One Week with the Green Bay Packers*, Reissue ed. (Simon & Schuster, 2014), 48.

for them. Last, there are the "pinnacle leaders," who are followed simply because of who they are and what they represent.[2]

All of us are somewhere within the spectrum of this leadership tier. As we ponder where we are in our level of leadership, let's ask ourselves, What will it take to move to the next level? And for those of us who think that we already are pinnacle leaders, think again. Very few people make it to this level of leadership, and when they do, it is typically later on in their career. I hope that all of us, including myself, can one day become a successful pinnacle leader.

If I were to be honest, I would say that I am in the early years of the people-development leadership stage. Over the past three to four years, I have recognized a change in my leadership from being the sole bottom-line producer in my ministry to now equipping others to participate in the production. I do not know that I will fully distance myself from being a producer because I love the work of ministry. It is fun and rewarding to me. But I cannot spend all or even a lot of my time leading from a production standpoint. In order for me to help others be successful and make a lasting impact on lives, I have to live my life every day looking at how I can equip and train others to do their best. That is the role that God has given to me now. That is why I am writing this book. Not only is it my calling to serve the church as a worship pastor and to equip people within my church and ministry to live successful lives as followers of Christ, but it is an extension of my calling to equip other worship leaders, church staff, businessmen and women, and families to be successful in their ministries, businesses, and homes.

At the beginning of this book, I shared with you my working definition of *success*, and throughout the chapters, I have

---

2   John C. Maxwell, *Developing the Leader Within You* (Grand Rapids, MI: Thomas Nelson, 2005).

unpackaged all the collective wisdom I have learned on my own ministry journey. In the end, success is not what we do but is who we are and what we help others become.

I am currently in a Bible study with one of my friends, and along with the Bible, we have been reading Tony Dungy's book *Quiet Strength*. Just a few weeks ago, we were in the middle of the Bible study using Tony's book when we came across a chapter with his definition of *success*. His definition resonated with me and was articulated so powerfully. I would like to finish this book with this excerpt from Tony Dungy:

> The competing views of success in our world often create an interesting tension. Society tends to define success in terms of accomplishments and awards, material possessions, and profit margins. In the football business, winning is the only thing that matters.
>
> God's Word, however, presents a different definition of success—one centered on a relationship with Jesus Christ and a love for God that allows us to love and serve others. God gives each one of us unique gifts, abilities, and passions. How well we use those qualities to have an impact on the world around us determines how "successful" we really are.
>
> If we get caught up in chasing what the world defines as success, we can use our time and talent to do some great things. We might even become famous. But in the end, what will it mean?
>
> What will people remember us for? Are other people's lives better because we lived? Did we make a difference? Did we use to the fullest the gifts and abilities God gave us? Did we give our best efforts, and did we do it for the right reasons?
>
> God's definition of success is really one of **significance**—the significant difference our lives can make in the lives of others. This significance doesn't show up in the win-loss records, long resumes, or the trophies gathering dust on our mantels. It's found in the hearts

and lives of those we've come across who are in some way better because of the way we lived.[3]

I urge us all to not insult our calling by merely surviving in this life and ministry. God has equipped us with all the tools that we need to be successful and even thrive. Christ did not die on the cross so that we might live mediocre and mundane lives. He came, died, and rose again so that we can be victors and live life in abundance and freedom and joy and peace. He never promised us that the journey would be easy or without pain, but He did promise us that He would never leave us or turn His back on us.

Finish this book with a new resolve about the future. Start today with a fresh perspective on the days ahead. We can begin to move from where we are right now with a commitment to seize God's future for our lives and ministries. He wants us to move toward the significant. No matter what size our organization is or where we are in our leadership journey—with Christ, there is a greater strength within all of us, one that is hardwired not for just survival but for great success! *Onward!*

Questions for Reflection

1. What type of a leader are you currently?
2. What will it take for you to move to the next level of leadership influence?
3. What do you need to do differently so that you can make steps toward your next level of leadership?

---

3   Tony Dungy with Nathan Whitaker, *Quiet Strength: the Principles, Practices and Priorities of a Winning Life* (Carol Stream, IL: Tyndale Momentum, 2008), 143-144.

Next Steps for Success

1. Ask someone close to you what kind of a leader they think you are. Allow them to help you honestly evaluate your leadership style and position.

2. Make a detailed list of the necessary steps to move to the next level of leadership or advancement from your current level.

3. Once you have accurately identified where you are as a leader, discuss your assessment with someone else. Let this person know of your desire to move forward.

4. Decide to be a person of influence and live a life of significance.